Soaring With PROPHECIES

How to experience the fulfillment of prophecies

MOSES UWABUN

SOARING

WITH

PROPHECIES

How to experience the fulfillment of prophecies

MOSES UWABUN

SOARING WITH PROPHECIES

Published and Printed in the United States by: Kingsworld Int'l
Ministry and Vision Directives www.VisionDirectives.com

Major Scripture: "See, the former things have taken place, and
new things I declare; before they spring into being I announce
them to you." (Isa.42:9)

ISBN: 9780578433646

Editor: Amos Aghemore I.
www.christiancopywritinghub.com/ christianfreelance247@gmail.com

CONTACTS:
KINGDOM AGENDA CHURCH
BALTIMORE MD 21229, USA
EMAIL: Philmosys07@gmail.com

KINGSWORLD INT'L MINISTRY
NO: 1 BETTER LIFE ARENA,
EVBUOTUBU 4 JUNCTION ,
BENIN CITY, EDO STATE, NIGERIA.
TEL: +2347033314606
EMAIL: philmosys07@gmail.com

CONTENTS

ACKNOWLEDGMENTS

To God; the Father of my Lord and Savior Jesus Christ, who knew me before He formed me in the womb, who set me apart for His purpose and anointed me with His Holy Spirit—the source of my inspirations. To Him I humbly, willfully, and joyfully give all glory, honor and praise.

I would like to express my gratitude to my peculiar treasure, my wife, the biological mother of my three children, my friend, the embodiment of God's favor, Philomena C. Uwabun, for her love and support all the way. I don't know what life and ministry would have been like without her. Indeed, she is the wind beneath my wings.

I would also like to thank Pastor Candice D. Owens, senior and founding pastor of Kingdom Agenda Church, USA for her sincerity, openness of heart, and absolute confidence in the Holy Spirit. And of course, all members of Kingdom Agenda Church (KAC).

Special thanks to Pastor Dan Aidellagbon and members of Kingsworld Int'l Ministry, Benin City, Nigeria, for your love for God, as well as your unwavering commitment and loyalty. You all are unique colors in my rainbow.

I would like to acknowledge my Spiritual fathers, Bishop Emmanuel E. Udah, and Apostle Ehimen C. Okhiria for their imparting on my life and ministry.

Many thanks also goes to my mother, Mrs. Agnes E. Uwabun, Eldest brother, Mr. Barry A. Uwabun, Parents in-laws, Pa And Ma Stephen Ogbogu, family members and friends who have all contributed to my life one way or the other.

My unreserved appreciation goes to Pastor (Dr.) James Adeoye for taking the time to read through the manuscripts, then make suggestions and contributions towards this publication.

I will not fail to acknowledge a father; who humbled himself to be a friend, whom I covet the grace and excellent spirit at work in his life, Pastor Johnson E. Iyere. Thanks for your prayer and motivations.

Finally; my sincere appreciation goes to Pastor Amos I. Aghemore for taking the time to edit this book; all my sons and daughters in ministry; my leaders and my followers...together we shall soar high.

Thanks, and God bless you all.

INTRODUCTION

"See, the former things have taken place, and new things I declare; before they spring into being I announce them to you." (Isa.42:9)

God always takes delight in telling and showing His people things ahead of time. Part of God's nature is His desire to communicate with man. Beginning with the first man in the Garden of Eden, God talked with man and it was natural for man to hear God.

> *Then the man and his wife heard the sound of the LORD God as he was walking in the garden in the cool of the day, and they hid from the LORD God among the trees of the garden. But the LORD God called to the man, "Where are you?" He answered, "I heard you in the garden, and I was afraid because I was naked; so I hid." And he said, "Who told you that you were naked? Have you eaten from the tree that I commanded you not to eat from?" The man said, "The woman you put here with me-- she gave me some fruit from the tree, and I ate it." Then the LORD God said to the woman, "What is this you have done?" The woman said, "The serpent deceived me, and I ate."* (Gen. 3:8-13)

The above verses of Scripture reveal the communication style God originally desired to have with man. It was a two–way communication where God the *sender* transmits a message to man the *receiver*. When the receiver *(man)* gets the message, he sends back a response, acknowledging the message was received.

There was no intermediary between God and man (Adam). Instead He came to man for fellowship. This event was not the first time God had fellowship with man. If it was, Adam would not have been able to identify the sound of God's movement and His voice when He called out to him. Previously, man-Adam was instructed to name all the creatures. He was instructed on what to eat in the garden and what not to eat. He was instructed to dress the garden and given all responsibilities and rules for living successfully by verbal communication from God.

Though the woman (Eve) was not yet created when most of these instructions were given, her response to God's question validated her familiarity with God's voice that could have only resulted from previous fellowship / communication. "*Then the LORD God said to the woman, 'What is this you have done?' The woman said, 'The serpent deceived me, and I ate'*" (Gen. 3:13).

Before Jesus Christ came to restore man back to God and give us the Holy Spirit, God spoke to His people through divinely chosen individuals who were set aside by God to receive a message from Him and speak to His people. These chosen individuals who were ordained or anointed to occupy the office of receiving messages from God and relaying them to His people were called prophets and the messages they conveyed were called prophecies.

Throughout the Old Testament, prophets were seen as intermediaries between God and the people. However, what is important to note is that prior to the law, God talked to Abraham, Isaac and Jacob directly without a seer or prophet.

The first mention of a prophet in the Bible was when God spoke to Abimelech, king of Gerar, in a dream, warning him concerning Sarai, Abram's wife whom he had taken to be his wife.

> *Then God said to him in the dream, "Yes, I know you did this with a clear conscience, and so I have kept you from sinning against me. That is why I did not let you touch her. Now return the man's wife, for he is a prophet, and he will pray for you and you will live. But if you do not return her, you may be sure that you and all who belong to you will die."* (Gen. 20:6-7)

Before the annunciation of Abraham's prophetic mantle, the divine criteria of being a prophet already existed. God knew that Abimelech understood what it meant to be a prophet, or else He would have had no need to mention this to him. That means that the divine authority backing a true prophet is recognized in all the earth. Hence, Abimelech, who was a pagan could respect that divine authority and restore the prophet's wife without harm. *"Now return the man's wife, for he is a prophet, and he will pray for you and you will live. But if you do not return her, you may be sure that you and all who belong to you will die"* (Gen. 20:8).

Though this book is not focused on who is a prophet or the authority of a prophet, but from what God said concerning Abraham; *"…and he will pray for you and you will live;"* does this means God honors a prophet's declarations and answers his or her prayers? If yes, are you a prophet in a way?

We live in a generation where people want to be assured of

positive outcomes for the decisions they make before venturing out. People want to be assured their marriages will succeed. Politicians want to be assured they will win the election even before ballots are cast. The list is unending. People incessantly obsess about what their future holds for them. This mindset has given rise to deceptions and manipulations by many who are not followers of Jesus Christ. These people prey on people's gullibility, robbing many of their precious destinies with the spirit of divination and soothsaying.

This book will emphasize and show you how to take advantage of the word of God (prophecy), using it like binoculars to view your future, stir your faith, command victory in all invisible battles, pattern your words in alignment with God's, generate corresponding actions towards the fulfilment of God's word concerning you, overcome the deceptions and manipulations of this age, and through God's word take advantage of the storm to soar high above the cloud like an eagle (See 2 Peter 1:19-21).

Our mind is programmed by our thoughts, which rules and directs our lives. Everyone's life moves in the direction of his or her dominant thoughts. This is a spiritual law. Hence, God gave us His word to renew and pattern our thoughts.

Notes

> . "I will stand at my watch and station myself on the ramparts; I will look to see what he will say to me, and what answer I am to give to this complaint. Habakkuk 2:1

Notes

_____

_____

_____

_____

_____

_____

_____

_____

_____

_____

CHAPTER ONE

PROPHETS AND PROPHECIES

"That is why I did not let you touch her. Now return the man's wife, for he is a prophet, and he will pray for you and you will live. But if you do not return her, you may be sure that you and all who belong to you will die" (Gen.20:7 NIV).

It is difficult to talk about prophecy without mentioning prophets. A prophet is one of the five-fold ministries (the five governmental offices of the body of Christ), and a prophet has the divine enablement to operate in any of these five-fold ministries as occasion demands.

A prophet admonishes, warns, encourages, directs, guides, teaches, counsels, and intercedes. The Prophet Samuel said it this way: *"As for me, far be it from me that I should sin against the LORD by failing to pray for you. And I will teach you the way that is good and right"* (1 Sam.12:23).

In simplest terms, a prophecy is something a prophet sees and says or declares. That is *prophe-see or prophe-say*. A good and scriptural definition of prophecy is found in Habakkuk 2:1. *"I will stand at my watch and station myself on the ramparts; I will look to see what he will say to me, and what answer I am to give to this complaint."* We can see from that Scripture that prophecy is hearing what God said and then saying it.

Another good and scriptural definition of prophecy is found

in Ezekiel 37:4. *"Then he said to me, 'Prophesy to these bones and say to them, Dry bones, hear the word of the LORD!'"* That means to hear God's voice and say what God said or to repeat after God.

> **"**
> Prophecy can be seen as God's specific inspired word, in specific human spirit, for a specific purpose, at a specific season, **"**

Again, Ezekiel 37:7 says: *"So I prophesied as I was commanded. And as I was prophesying, there was a noise, a rattling sound, and the bones came together, bone to bone."* From Ezekiel's account, it is clear that prophesying is simply saying what God asks you to say, either to yourself, a person, a group of people, a nation, a government or even dry bones. This means prophecy is not saying what you like, nor is it saying what you think the people want to hear. It is saying what God said.

Although prophecy is often about the future, it is not a prediction or forecasting like many think. **Prophecy is certain, sure, reliable, confirmed, true, firm…and because only God's word has these characteristics,** *prophecy can be seen as God's specific inspired word, in specific human spirit, for a specific purpose, at a specific season, to specific person, people or situation(s) to lead, guide, encourage and even warn His people, or other nations what He will do in the future.*

Second Peter 1:19-21 declares *"We also have the prophetic message as something completely reliable* (sure word, strongly confirmed, confirmed beyond a doubt, altogether reliable, more certain, true word, firmer), *and you will do well to pay attention to it, as to a light shining in a dark place, until the day dawns and the morning star rises in your hearts. Above all, you must understand that no prophecy of Scripture came about by the prophet's own interpretation of things. For prophecy never had its origin in the human will, but prophets, though human, spoke from God as they were carried along by the Holy Spirit"* (emphasis mine).

Prophecy is not saying premeditated words, nor speaking enticing words of man's wisdom. It's speaking Holy Spirit inspired words that can be used to give direction, warning, instruction, correction, teaching, rebuke, comfort, and encouragement, to build hope and stir faith, and call for repentance.

According to Apostle Paul; prophecy is for edification, exhortation, and comfort. But the one who prophesies speaks to people for their strengthening, encouraging and comfort. Anyone who speaks in a tongue edifies themselves, but the one who prophesies edifies the church (1 Cor.14:3-4).

> **"** ..Prophecy is not saying premeditated words, nor speaking enticing words of man's wisdom., **"**

He gives one person the power to perform miracles, and another the ability to prophesy... (1Cor.12:10).

Again, Paul said in 1 Cor. 14:1,5,31 to *"Follow the way of love and eagerly desire gifts of the Spirit, especially prophecy...I wish you could all speak in tongues, but even more I wish you could all prophesy...For you can all prophesy in turn so that everyone may be instructed and encouraged."*

This makes it clear that every believer can prophecy. Just as there are prophets to nations (Major Prophets), there are also prophets to states, communities, and families (Minor Prophets).

Every believer is a prophet of his or her own destiny.

ABRAHAM, THE FIRST PROPHET

Many people do not generally associate Abraham as being among the Old Testament prophets, primarily because there was no record of him delivering messages time and time again, speaking "Thus said the Lord…" Yet, he is the first man to be called a prophet by God in the Bible. Therefore, according to the law of first mention, Abraham, the first prophet, has all the criteria for being a prophet.

For further understanding and re-definition of the functions of a prophet, the prophetic life of Abraham is worthy of examination.

ABRAHAM, GOD'S MOUTHPIECE: God called Abraham, told him WHERE to go and WHAT He would do to bless him for his obedience. Abraham was God's spokesperson.

Now [in Haran] the Lord had said to Abram, "Go away from your country, And from your relatives. And from your father's house, To the land which I will show you; And I will make you a great nation, And I will bless you [abundantly], And make your name great (exalted, distinguished); And you shall be a blessing [a source of great good to others]; And I will bless (do good for, benefit) those who bless you, And I will curse [that is, subject to My wrath and judgment] the one who curses (despises, dishonors, has contempt for) you. And in you all the families (nations) of the earth will be blessed." So Abram departed [in faithful obedience] as the Lord had directed him; and Lot [his nephew] left with him. Abram was seventy-five years old when he left Haran. (Gen.12:1-4 AMP)

> **"** ..Prophecy is certain, sure, reliable, confirmed, true, firm...and because only God's word has these characteristics, **"**

God didn't just call Abraham (or Abram), he heard and responded to God accordingly. Abraham heard God's message concerning his life, his family, and his future. At this point Abram was God's spokesman (prophet) to the other members of his family. By this prophecy, Abraham decided both his future and that of the family members he knew and loved. There was no record of other miracles performed by Abram either before or after this prophecy to convince his wife and family members. This could be evidence that his words came with demonstration of the Spirit and the power of almighty God. In other words, because his words received God's backing, there were no human efforts to try and persuade others to believe and follow him.

ABRAHAM, THE INTERCESSION: Prophets do not only give warning; they also intercede in attempts to reverse possible danger. Abraham interceded.

> *So the men turned from there and went toward Sodom, but Abraham still stood before the Lord. Then Abraham drew near and said, "Will you indeed sweep away the righteous with the wicked? Suppose there are fifty righteous within the city. Will you then sweep away the place and not spare it for the fifty righteous who are in it? Far be it from you*

to do such a thing, to put the righteous to death with the wicked, so that the righteous fare as the wicked! Far be that from you! Shall not the Judge of all the earth do what is just?" And the Lord said, "If I find at Sodom fifty righteous in the city, I will spare the whole place for their sake. "Abraham answered and said, "Behold, I have undertaken to speak to the Lord, I who am but dust and ashes. Suppose five of the fifty righteous are lacking. Will you destroy the whole city for lack of five?" And he said, "I will not destroy it if I find forty-five there." Again he spoke to him and said, "Suppose forty are found there." He answered, "For the sake of forty I will not do it." Then he said, "Oh let not the Lord be angry, and I will speak. Suppose thirty are found there." He answered, "I will not do it, if I find thirty there." He said, "Behold, I have undertaken to speak to the Lord. Suppose twenty are found there." He answered, "For the sake of twenty I will not destroy it." Then he said, "Oh let not the Lord be angry, and I will speak again but this once. Suppose ten are found there." He answered, "For the sake of ten I will not destroy it." And the Lord went his way, when he had finished speaking to Abraham, and Abraham returned to his place. (Gen.18:22-33)

ABRAHAM PROPHESIED: Prophets say things that are yet to happen and Abraham did just that.

He said to his servants, "Stay here with the donkey while I and the boy go over there. ***"We will worship and then we will come back to you"*** (Gen.22:5, Emphasis mine).

This was a prophetic declaration. He never thought on how he would explain it to his servant if he didn't come back with Isaac his son. He was so persuaded and consumed with doing what God said, his mind left no room for any possible alternative.

Again, Abraham prophesied the birth of Jesus Christ to his son Isaac when he answered Isaac thus: *"Isaac spoke up and said to his father Abraham, "Father?" "Yes, my son?" Abraham replied. "The fire and wood are here," Isaac said, "but where is the lamb for the burnt offering? Abraham said,* **"God will provide for himself the lamb for a burnt offering, my son.** *" So they went both of them together"* (Gen. 22:7-8, ESV, Emphasis mine).

This prophecy went beyond the immediate lamb used in the place of Isaac to refer to the lamb who was slain for the whole world. Jesus is the lamb Abraham prophesied of. John the Baptist confirmed this in the New Testament. *"The next day he saw Jesus coming toward him, and said, "Behold, the Lamb of God, who takes away the sin of the world!"* (John 1:29, ESV). Prophecy is not only about doom, danger, or evil. Prophecy can be about peace, joy, welfare, success, grace, or righteousness... Hallelujah!

TEACHING AND WARNING: A prophet is a teacher. He explains God's word and warns against danger or the consequences of violating God's order. Abraham was also a trainer. *"For I know him, that he will command his children and his household after him, and they shall keep the way of the LORD, to do justice and judgment; that the LORD may bring upon Abraham that which he hath spoken of him"* (Gen. 18:19, KJV). God trusted Abraham so much that He knew he would teach God's word to his children and all connected to him (See also Gen. 14:14).

7

KNOWLEDGE OF GOD'S PLANS AND
PURPOSE:"Surely the Sovereign LORD does nothing without revealing his plan to his servants the prophets." (Amos 3:7).

"Then the LORD said, 'Shall I hide from Abraham what I am about to do? (Gen.18:17). The principle of God is to reveal His plans to His prophet ahead of time. And because Abraham was His prophet, the future plan against Sodom and Gomorrah was not hidden from him.

In another situation, God also told Abraham his descendants would become slaves in Egypt, and thereafter they will come out with great possession. These future events were unfolded to Abraham because He was a prophet. *"Then the LORD said to him, 'Know for certain that for four hundred years your descendants will be strangers in a country not their own and that they will be enslaved and mistreated there. But I will punish the nation they serve as slaves, and afterward they will come out with great possessions.'"* (Gen.15:13).

> **..Thoughts of mediocrity makes one mediocre. Corrupt thoughts corrupt one's life and destiny.**

WORSHIP AND SACRIFICE: *"Abraham looked up and there in a thicket he saw a ram caught by its horns. He went over and took the ram and sacrificed it as a burnt offering instead of his son"* (Gen. 22:13). Sacrifice is an act of worship unto God.

In addition to the above prophetic functions, Abraham, also fought wars (See Gen.14:14-17).

Abraham saw and declared the future, calling those things that were not as if they were.

There are many other functions of a prophet that are not

explained in this book. The prophetic functions listed are not more important than the ones not listed. This author's choice to focus on prophesy is to concentrate on showing you how to make prophecy come to fruition in your life. When the "how" to any situation or problem is not known, solutions remains elusive, efforts turn futile, life becomes experiments, expectations end in disappointment, and quitting becomes imminent. So it is, when the knowledge of how to make prophecy a reality is lacking.

Our mind is programmed by our thoughts, which rules and directs our lives. Everyone's life moves in the direction of his or her dominant thoughts. This is a spiritual law. Hence, God gave us His word to renew and pattern our thoughts.

Notes

CHAPTER TWO

WHY PROPHECIES

"See, the former things have taken place, and new things I declare; before they spring into being I announce them to you." (Isa. 42:9 NIV)

The Prophet Isaiah said, the older prophecies have happened. But even today, God is still purposely committed to telling/showing His people things regarding their future ahead of time.

Basically, God's purpose for telling us things ahead of time is to prepare and guide us into the fulfillment of the prophecy. Preparation involves revealing what to do to avert judgment or receive the blessing if it is a conditional proph-ecy. If it is an absolute prophecy, preparation will keep our hope alive, program our mind, and make us dependent on Him who promised so that at the end we will give Him the glory due to His name.

Now, let us look a little more into the two types of prophecies mentioned above.

ABSOLUTE PROPHECIES: These are prophecies which have no condition(s) attached to their fulfillment. They do not require any human intervention. Human activities do not in any way determine or prevent their fulfillment. This type of prophecy does not necessarily require prayer to see the fulfillment, nor can prayer stop the fulfillment. They are God's divine agenda which will, of a certainty, manifest itself with time. The best humans can do is to seek exemption. There are many such prophecies in the Bible. For instance, there is nothing anyone can do or will not do to stop rumors of war, nations fighting against nations or famine, nor stop the church of Jesus Christ from radiating the glory of the Lord when gross darkness has taken over the Earth. *So when you see standing in the holy place 'the abomination of desolation,' described by the prophet Daniel (let the reader understand)* (Matt.24:15).

CONDITIONAL PROPHECY: This type of prophecy has conditions which must be fulfilled for one to see the fulfillment. Most of the time, they are open to whoever meets the conditions. For instance, *"if you fully obey the LORD your God and carefully follow all his commands I give you today, the LORD your God will set you high above all the nations on earth"* (Deut.28:1). Obedience to the commandment determines who will be the head and the tail, who will be a lender and not a borrower.

So, why prophecies?

1. **To program your mind**: Mind programming is one of the primary reasons God speaks or show us things ahead of time. God's desire is that we program our mind and pattern our thoughts after His word. This is important because the totality of a man is a function of his mind. The apostle Paul said, *"But I did not want to do anything without your consent* (mind), *so that any favor you do would not seem forced but would be voluntary"* (Phlm.1:14).

The power of your mind cannot be fully explained. But

programming your mind is so important that God has to warn us to put on all efforts or work very hard to protect it. This is because whatever we accept into our mind determines the overall outcome of our lives. *"Watch over your heart with all diligence* (work hard), *for from it flow the springs of life"* (Prov.4:23 NASB. Emphasis mine). Whoever you open your heart for has your heart, and whoever has your heart becomes your master.

> "..Thoughts of mediocrity makes one mediocre. Corrupt thoughts corrupt one's life and destiny..,"

✡

Our mind is programmed by our thoughts, which rules and directs our lives. Everyone's life moves in the direction of his or her dominant thoughts. This is a spiritual law. Hence, God gave us His word to renew and pattern our thoughts. The mind receives information, processes / analyzes information, converts information, stores information, and transmits information. Here's what the Scripture said of Mary the mother of Jesus in this regard: *"But Mary treasured* (stored) *up all these things and pondered them in her heart*" (Luke 2:19, 49-51). There were times when Mary didn't understood what was said, yet she stored it in her mind for further processing.

Again, we see from scriptures that Jacob did the same thing when Joseph told of his family about his dream that they would one day bow down before him: *"His brothers were jealous of him, but his father kept the matter in mind*" (Gen. 37:11). Truly the mind can be set (programmed), be unset (deprogrammed), and be reset (reprogrammed), *"Those who live according to the flesh have their minds SET* (programmed) *on what the flesh desires; but*

> **❝** ..All our actions are products of our thoughts. Our thoughts determine our destiny and our destiny determines our legacy. **❞**

those who live in accordance with the Spirit have their minds SET (programmed) *on what the Spirit desires* (Rom. 8:5, Emphasis mine). Whatever the mind is set on (programmed) is what the mind will process. What the mind processes is what the mind will produce. What the mind produces is your character and your character is who you are. Hear this: *"For as he thinks within himself, so he is. He says to you, "Eat and drink!" But his heart is not with you"* (Prov. 23:7, NASB).

God wants us to think His word because what we think determines who we are and who we are determines what we do. All our actions are products of our thoughts. Our thoughts determine our destiny and our destiny determines our legacy. Where you are today is the place where your thoughts have brought you and tomorrow you will be where your thoughts take you. God said to Joshua, think on the word alone night and day and your success will be inevitable. (See Josh. 1:8, Phil. 4:8, and Jer. 29:11).

Whatever captures your mind makes you a captive, whether good or bad. People who seek after the fulfillment of God's word think differently from others. Small/negative thinking limits achievements while big/good thinking expands possibilities. A person who thinks, doesn't sink. Only people who see themselves going far, think far. Thinking influences your behavior and your response to situations.

Let me ask you this question: If God knows the thoughts He has for you in life, what thoughts do you have towards yourself?

14

Think on that! This is so important because one of the ways God can make His good thoughts towards you come through, is to first make you think good thoughts about yourself. *"Don't copy the behavior and customs of this world, but let God transform you into a new person by changing the way you think. Then you will learn to know God's will for you, which is good and pleasing and perfect"* (Rom.12:2, NLT). When you change your way of thinking, your way of living will change. And when you change your way of living, your overall outcome will change.

Friends, what God said to Joshua, He is saying to all who believe. Dedicate your time to meditating on God's words until they becomes the dominant thoughts that rule your life. This is a step to making prophecies a reality in your life. Think of Elevation, Better life, Success, Health, Righteousness, Love, things that are True, Pure and Praise worthy, and of Good report...(Phil.4:8). Poor thoughts make one poor. Thoughts of mediocrity makes one mediocre. Corrupt thoughts corrupt one's life and destiny.

> **"** ..When you change your way of thinking, your way of living will change. And when you change your way of living, your overall outcome will change. **"**

The Scripture says: *"Moreover the profit of the earth is for all..."* (Eccl.5:9). This Bible verse consumed me so much in my early life far back in my Polytechnic days that I started a "Billionaire Club." Although no physical cash was present, we achieved our goal of helping others who were financially disadvantaged. To date everyone who bought into that vision are doing well in life. My point is: You are what you think. To become what God

> ".. To become what God said, think what God said. Don't accept any of the devil's suggestions that negates God's word concerning your life.."

said, think what God said. Don't accept any of the devil's suggestions that negates God's word concerning your life. Thoughts of fear, anger, depression, idleness, immorality, poverty, laziness, rejection...are enemies of productivity and as such they should be cast down immediately (See 2 Cor. 10:5).

2. **To influence your words**: Your thoughts are revealed in your words. Every man speaks what his mind is programmed to do...which is another reason why God speaks to us ahead of time. *"A good man brings good things out of the good stored up in his heart, and an evil man brings evil things out of the evil stored up in his heart. For the mouth speaks what the heart is full of"* Luke.6:45. God wants your words to be in alignment with His because your words create your world. You can make or mar your destiny with your words. About six hundred thousand men, besides women and children, terminated their destiny in the wilderness because they murmured (that is speaking contrary to what God said). *"The Israelites journeyed from Rameses to Sukkoth. There were about six hundred thousand men on foot, besides women and children"* (Ex.12:37). It is suicidal to say you are not able when God says you are. *"How long will this wicked community grumble against me? I have heard the complaints of these grumbling Israelites.* **So tell them, 'As surely as I live, declares the LORD, I will do to you the very thing I heard you say**: *In this wilderness your bodies will fall--every one of you twenty years old or more who was counted in the census and who has grumbled against me. Not one of you will enter the land I swore with uplifted hand to make your home, except Caleb son of*

Jephunneh and Joshua son of Nun. As for your children that you said would be taken as plunder, I will bring them in to enjoy the land you have rejected. But as for you, your bodies will fall in this wilderness" (Numb.14:27-32). Also see Numb.13:25-33. There is no place **for** rebels in God's agenda, and not agreeing with God's word makes you a rebel. **Grumbling is** any words we say that opposes or disagrees with God's. By prophecy, God is attempting to influence our corrupt words to align with His, and thereby make us a qualified candidate for the glorious land flowing with milk and honey He has prepared and prophesied to us. Our best friends are people who speak our language or share a common language. God wants us to speak His language, not our experience or what we see. He wants us to always speak the promise, not the process. He wants us to speak the blessing, not the challenges. Your words either associate or disassociate you from the promise. In fact, prophesy is speaking or saying what God said after you heard God.

> **There is no place for rebels in God's agenda, and not agreeing with God's word makes you a rebel.**

For instance, God asked Ezekiel to prophesy to the dry bones: *"Then he said to me, 'Prophesy to these bones and say to them, 'Dry bones, hear the word of the LORD!'"* (Ez. 37:4). Ezekiel went ahead and did what God said to him. Ezekiel was actually repeating after God. God told him what to say and in verse 7 of the same chapter, Ezekiel said: *"So I prophesied as I was commanded. And as I was prophesying, there was a noise, a rattling sound, and the bones came together, bone to bone."* Simply put, Ezekiel repeated what he heard God say. God wants us to speak His word at all times to every situation.

At the creation, God modeled the perfect example of how we should speak or prophesy His word to our situations. He saw darkness and emptiness, instead He spoke light and abundance to being. *"Now the earth was formless and empty, darkness was over the surface of the deep, and the Spirit of God was hovering over the waters. And God said, 'Let there be light," and there was light'"* (Genesis 1:2-3, NASB). Take a clue from God.

For 25 years, Abraham believed God and continually spoke the prophecy of God over his life, ignoring the prevailing circumstances. No situation has the capacity to endure forever like God's word. *"As it is written: 'I have made you a father of many nations.' He is our father in the sight of God, in whom he believed--the God who gives life to the dead and calls into being things that were not"* (Rom 4:17).

As free as salvation is, it's not complete if you only believe in your heart without confession with your mouth. Confession is an expression of your faith. If you cannot confess the prophecy you may not see the manifestation. Saying it is sealing it. The more you say it, the more you want to know about it, and the more you know about it, the more meaning it makes to you, and the higher your expectations.

3. To guide your studies and search. God doesn't want you confused. God doesn't want you stranded; neither does He want you frustrated. The lack of adequate knowledge can be frustrating. It's one thing to hear God; it's another to understand the details. The details are communicated through a deliberate search to learn more. If what is said cannot be confirmed with what is written, then what is said may be doubted.

We understand from Scripture that Jesus discovered more about Himself through studies. It was His usual habit to read scripture scrolls. In one of the instances, Jesus found the place where it was written concerning Him. So, "find" suggests he searched... *"He went to Nazareth, where he had been brought up, and on the Sabbath day he went into the synagogue, as was his custom. He stood up to read and the scroll of the prophet Isaiah was handed to him. Unrolling it, he found the place where it is written; 'The Spirit of the Lord is on me, because he has anointed me to proclaim good news to the poor. He has sent me to proclaim freedom for the prisoners and recovery of sight for the blind, to set the oppressed free, to proclaim the year of the Lord's favor'"* (Luke 4:16-19).

If you don't know what is written, what is said may be of no value to you. What is written, validates what is said. And in most cases, what is written overrules what is said. That is why partnership agreements, wills, or testaments are written and not just said. **Jesus capitalized on the power of the written word to overrule Satan's suggestions and to overcome temptations**.

Prophecy can define the scope of studies. The conditions to fulfilling prophecy will be unfolded when you engage in a deliberate search, according to the prophecy you received. Remember, the more you know, the more freedom you will enjoy. *"Then you will know the truth, and the truth will set you free"* (John 8:32).

In addition to knowing the conditions, possible self-imposed hindrances will also be revealed. For instance, the Scripture says; *"Well then, should we keep on sinning so that God can show us more and more of his wonderful grace? Of course not! Since we have died to sin, how can we continue to live in it?"* (Rom. 6:1-2, NLT). Sin in this context is doing the opposite of what is required. Can I remain idle or lazy and expect God to bless me? Of course not! Should I remain unfaithful and expect more blessings? Of course not! God's word cannot be broken. Can I live a life of unforgiveness and expect prayers to be answered? Of course not! The word is clear: *"Whenever you stand praying, forgive, if you have anything against anyone; so that your Father, who is in heaven, may also forgive you your transgressions. But if you do not forgive, neither will your Father in heaven forgive your transgressions"* (Matt. 11:25-26).

> **"** When you are under a prophetic guide, you don't read anything, you don't listen to anything, but your study is guided by the prophecy over your life. **"**

When you are under a prophetic guide, you don't read anything, you don't listen to anything, but your study is guided by the prophecy over your life. When God promises you fruitfulness, you study in that direction to know more. Every prophecy leaves you with a responsibility. Though prosperity is God's upmost priority for believers, every believer has the responsibility to search for the core principles of prosperity and apply him/ herself to them. If not, that promise will remain noting more than a theory. This applies to every prophecy/promise from God.

4. **To stir your faith:** What you hear will either build your faith or create fear. *"Consequently, faith comes from hearing the message, and the message is heard through the word about Christ"* (Rom.10:17). Among all things, prophecy is to boost your confidence in God and eliminate the fear of the unknown. No true prophecy is designed to make you fear, instead it is designed to increase your reverence for God. While faith is confidence in God and His word (in spite of the enemies and prevailing situations), fear is confidence in the enemy's abilities (in spite of God's promises). To be overwhelmed by these opinions is worry. In this regard, prophecy helps to direct your confidence, enhance focus and overcome fear. When you focus on what God said about your future, joy will fill your heart and there will be no space for fear and anxiety. But if your faith is not stirred to praise and thank God and possibly pray, either you did not hear God, or you did not understand God, or both.

The knowledge of God's plan for your future should motivate you to do things positively different. Faith makes you do things you would not have done and stops you from doing things you should have naturally done. Faith changed Joseph's plan of secret divorce to a public wedding. If what you are hearing cannot change you, change what you are hearing.

> **"**..Among all things, prophecy is to boost your confidence in God and eliminate the fear of the unknown. **"**

"Because Joseph her husband was faithful to the law, and yet did not want to expose her to public disgrace, he had in mind to divorce her quietly. But after he had considered this, an angel of the Lord

appeared to him in a dream and said, 'Joseph son of David, do not be afraid to take Mary home as your wife, because what is conceived in her is from the Holy Spirit... When Joseph woke up, he did what the angel of the Lord had commanded him and took Mary home as his wife'" (Matt.1:19-24). Faith is what gives you energy in prayer, joy in praise, and consistency in obedience.

Sometime ago, on my way to church, I came across a brother who is a member of our church. We greeted each other, and he told me he was getting ready to attend services that morning. To my amazement, after the service I never saw this brother. On my way home, I decided to check on him. I found out that he had gotten sick. This brother managed to tell me how this recurring illness has been a setback to his progress. He said, "This sickness always attacked me when I'm about to attain progress. And because of this I have missed several opportunities in life. I should have been better than this." After I prayed and left for home, I told him, "You are healed permanently today."

About five minutes after I got into my house, there was a knock on my door. It was this brother with bottles of drinks in his hands. He said to me: "Pastor, I am celebrating my healing. This is your drink...my friends are all celebrating with me." He anchored his faith and celebrated the word "you are healed permanently today" because he knew what that illness cost him. To the glory of God, he has never been sick since then. Be it prayer, praise, thanksgiving...anything not done in faith is a sin (See Rom. 14:23).

The prophetic is to draw you closer to God in fellowship, so you can trust Him more. And the truth is, God wants us to trust Him more. *"Let us hold fast the confession of our hope without wavering, for he who promised is faithful"* (Heb. 10:23). Faith determines the performance and fulfilment of prophecies (Lu. 1:45).

5. To give you expectation and focus: God is a jealous God. It grieves His heart when we wave and shift our focus from Him. He tells us things that lie ahead to win our focus. Before the storm ever starts, He has promised you safety, so you can trust Him and expect safety when it eventually comes.

Prophecy or no prophecy, there will always be storms. But your focus determines your end result. Peter walked on water until he lost focus. *"'Come,' he said. Then Peter got down out of the boat, walked on the water and came toward Jesus. But when he saw the wind, he was afraid and, beginning to sink, cried out, 'Lord, save me!'"* (Matt. 14:29-40). Peter only saw the wind after he took his focus from Jesus who called him. **Don't lose focus on the word; focus on what has been told to you. When focus is lost, expectation is dead. When there is no expectation, there will not be a manifestation.** God wants us to be blind to things and situations capable of stealing our focus, and expect the fulfilment of His word in our lives because His plan is to give us what we expect. God said though you may hear or see calamity, harm, and disaster, never focus on these things. They are just dust, meant to distract you from the real promise. *"For I know the plans I have for you,' declares the LORD, 'plans to prosper you and not to harm you, plans to give you hope and a future'"* (Jer. 29:11). When you understand that God's plans are not evil, you will always be focused and expect a good end to every situation that may come your way. Remember what Elijah told Elisha: *"'You have asked a difficult thing,' Elijah said, 'yet if you see me when I am taken from you, it will be yours--otherwise, it will not'"* (2Kings 2:10). What he is saying is focusing in the midst of possible distraction is a vital condition to turning expectation into experience.

6. **To empower you for warfare:** Prophecy does not mean life will always be rosy. But it does mean the enemy will get angrier and want to frustrate the prophecy. Prior to Jesus being publicly endorsed by the Holy Spirit, Satan never sought his downfall. *"And a voice from heaven said, 'This is my Son, whom I love; with him I am well pleased.' Then Jesus was led by the Spirit into the wilderness to be tempted by the devil"* (Matt.4:1).

Job was not attacked until God boasted about him. *"Then the LORD said to Satan, 'Have you considered my servant Job? There is no one on earth like him; he is blameless and upright, a man who fears God and shuns evil'"* (Job 1:8). The prophecy on your life can attract attacks from hell, not necessarily against you as it were, but against the prophecy of God for your life. However, your consolation is: *"Many are the plans in the mind of a man,* (and mind of the devil) *but it is the purpose of the LORD that will stand"* (Prov.19:21, emphasis added).

Every promised land is never a vacant land. Giants will always be there to contest your possession of it. If you are not ready to fight, you may not be able to possess your possession. Possessing usually occurs after battling. This is how the Scripture puts it: *"Set out now and cross the Arnon Gorge. See, I have given into your hand Sihon the Amorite, king of Heshbon, and his country. Begin to take possession of it and engage him in battle*" (Deut. 2:24).

Prophecies give you confidence to face any opposition that may be coming your way to hinder. Through prayer and warfare, you remind the devil of your expectation, and your destination, and that you have not and will not give up. Prayer is your proof of faith in God and in the prophecy. Warfare is both in words (prayer) and in deeds (action/behavior). (I will talk more about this in a later chapter).

7. **To motivate you to action:** Every prophecy when understood leaves the recipient(s) with responsibilities. And until what to do is known and done, prophecy may never be fulfilled. Those who take responsibility are blessed, not just the hearer. "*Do not merely listen to the word, and so deceive yourselves. Do what it says. Anyone who listens to the word but does not do what it says is like someone who looks at his face in a mirror and, after looking at himself, goes away and immediately forgets what he looks like. But whoever looks intently into the perfect law that gives freedom, and continues in it--not forgetting what they have heard, but doing it--they will be blessed in what they do*" (Jam.1:22-25 NIV).

Anybody can hear prophecy. In fact, God speaks to His people every day. But only those who take responsibility will see the fulfilment. Nothing happens to something you do nothing about, and that includes prophecy. That is why the best prayer is what Paul prayed when he encountered Jesus Christ. Paul said: "*My companions saw the light, but they did not understand the voice of him who was speaking to me. 'What shall I do, Lord?' I asked. 'Get up,' the Lord said, 'and go into Damascus. There you will be told all that you have been assigned to do'''* (Acts 22:9-10). That makes it simpler. The people with Paul did not understand the voice, only he did, only he acted and only he stood out.

Hearing alone is never enough until it's converted into action. When I understood this, after each teaching, I made my brethren sit quietly for few minutes to formulate an action plan in line with what they just heard. What you do determines what comes back to you.

A man had food and he kept saying, "I believed if I eat this food I will not die but live." He kept saying it repeatedly for days but never ate the food. He died of hunger and starvation after many days. Have you not heard? *"The labor of the foolish wearieth every one of them, because he knoweth not how to go to the city"* (Eccl.10:15 KJV). According to Matt. 7:26, foolishness is failure or refusal to act on the word. *"But everyone who hears these words of mine and does not put them into practice is like a foolish man who built his house on sand."*

When you fellowship with God in prayer, you receive insights or prophesy; you clear off the oppositions on your way to success; you receive the action plan and are empowered to act.

> **44** .. Through prayer and warfare, you remind the devil of your expectation, and your destination, and that you have not and will not give up. **77**

God said to Joshua, the reason for speaking and meditating on the word of prophecy is so you will know what to do. It is only by doing the word you will make your way prosperous and have good success (Josh.1:8). That tells me, though there may be delay and challenges; nothing can successfully stop the believer who is engaged in working God's word.

Prophecy, either through teaching, preaching, revelation, word of knowledge, or word of wisdom…are for us and our children to do. "*The secret (not prophesied yet) things belong to the LORD our God, but the things that are revealed (prophesied) belong to us and to our children forever, that we may do all the words of this law.*" (Deut.29:29 ESV. Emphasis mine).

The fifth book of the New Testament is called The Acts of the Apostles. It means the doings or demonstrations or actions of the Apostles. The first verse of the first chapter reads: "*In my former book, Theophilus, I wrote about all that Jesus began to do and to* teach." It was first what Jesus did before what he taught. God's word will always work for those who work it. The word that will not motivate you to action may not profit you. The word of God are instructions meant to be worked out.

The manifestation of the above said characteristics regarding the "why" of prophecies is a strong indication that you should believe in the word of prophecy spoken in your direction. If prophecy does not draw you closer to God and to do the "why" of prophecies as stated above, then you may want to examine the state of your heart to see if you understand what is being spoken to you, if you believe in it, or prove the prophecy. Faith is your prophet and the prophecy is a prerequisite to seeing the manifestations. The glory of the word is an exclusive reservation to those who believe (John 11:40).

> *Prophecy, either through teaching, preaching, revelation, word of knowledge, or word of wisdom...are for us and our children to do.*

📋 *Notes*

CHAPTER THREE

WINGS OF PROPHECIES

"You yourselves have seen what I did to Egypt, and how I carried you on eagles' wings and brought you to myself" (Ex.19:4).

"Remember what it says: "Today when you hear his voice, don't harden your hearts as Israel did when they rebelled" (Heb. 3:15).

From the beginning of creation God has always desired to talk with and to His children more than we desire to hear Him. In Genesis 2:9 it says God "brought them [the animals] unto Adam to see what he would call them."

This is a verse that is easy to gloss over but it's really amazing when we stop to meditate on it. *Colossians 1:17* states that "by him all things consist." Not only did God create all things, he still takes an active role making sure everything runs smoothly. Despite having a universe to run, God took an active interest in what Adam wanted to call each animal. This shows just how much God yearns to have a personal relationship with us.

If we don't have this relationship the problem is not with God, it is with us. One of our limitations is our mindset. We want God to speak to us on our terms and insist that he conform to our dictates. Some people have a preferred format or style they use to communicate with God. Whichever it is, for many, if God does not communicate with them using their preferred style they are not able or are unwilling to hear him.

A loving relationship utilizes a variety of methods to share the desires of the heart. My relationship with my wife is such that, regardless of which communication style I adopt at any given moment, she can hear me, identify my voice, and understand me.

I don't have to always introduce myself to her and remind her of who I am before sharing my message. Sometimes, there are no formal greetings; just the mention of her name is enough. Other times, just my speaking is enough for her to know I am talking to her. The same goes for my children and some friends I am very familiar with.

All of my friends have different names for me, but if any of them writes me a letter and forgets to sign their name, the wording and sentence structure alone is enough to tell me the source of that letter. To illustrate, consider those in our phone contacts; wouldn't it be strange if they started every conversation with a self-introduction?

We have missed out on God's guidance owing to a lack of intimacy with Him. God doesn't have a particular format of talking to His children to the exclusion of all others, but whichever method He uses, the Bible says we will know His voice. Irrespective of the method He used to talk with you this morning, He wants all of His children to grow up to develop a level of spiritual maturity and intimacy, enabling us to hear Him in the way a son hears his father and as sheep hear their shepherd. *"My sheep hear my voice, and I know them, and they follow me"* (John.10:27).

Prophecy is not just something you hear from another person (though the voice of God can be heard through another man's vocal cords). Prophecies come through the pages of His word, through direct witness to your Spirit, and so on. Some people only identify prophecy when someone starts shouting in the midst of prayers or worship, calling their name or shouting 'my children' repeatedly during an interlude of speaking in tongues or crying "thus says the Lord," or behaving as if he/she is unconscious. This mindset is wrong and can pose limitations to hearing from God. Not only that, by limiting yourself to these methods, it could leave you open to being misled or deceived (1 Ki. 13). Bear in mind, only a stubborn child makes his father yell at them.

Now, let us look at some ways God speaks to us.

1. **The written Word:** Void of personal interpretation, the Bible is a book of the most reliable, consistent, guaranteed, specific, simple, and clear prophecies. The written Word (Bible) is the standard and final authority for judging other forms of prophecies and is an open prophecy to whoever believes it. The written Word (Bible) becomes prophecy when the Holy Spirit illuminates your mind with it regarding an issue (Ps. 119:18). That illumination by the Holy Spirit means being personally persuaded beyond a doubt that what is written is yours. It is

making Scripture personal by faith.

In Luke 4:16-20, we see Jesus taking the written word personally, being persuaded completely that what was written was directed to Him:

> *He went to Nazareth, where he had been brought up, and on the Sabbath day he went into the synagogue, as was his custom. He stood up to read, and the scroll of the prophet Isaiah was handed to him. Unrolling it, he found the place where it is written: "The Spirit of the Lord is on me, because he has anointed me to proclaim good news to the poor. He has sent me to proclaim freedom for the prisoners and recovery of sight for the blind, to set the oppressed free, to proclaim the year of the Lord's favor." Then he rolled up the scroll, gave it back to the attendant and sat down. The eyes of everyone in the synagogue were fastened on him.*

It's important to note that it was Jesus' custom to read the scroll, and He might have read other verses before He found the ones that spoke to Him. He personalized the reading with his mannerism and gesticulation with such vigor that it caught the attention of everyone in the synagogue. I also suppose he added some drama in a way nobody had ever done before, to such an extent that everyone present could believe that he had truly read the prophecy about Himself.

Just like in our local churches today, it was possible that this particular Scripture had been read many times in the past in that synagogue. Perhaps he allowed for a prolonged pause after reading the text before saying, "*Today this scripture is fulfilled in your hearing*" (Luke 4:21).

Every spoken prophecy is either a direct or indirect inspiration from the written Word. I first understood this when I began my faith walk with God while in fasting and prayer, requesting God to speak to me. The very first word I ever heard from God as a baby Christian was: *"you can't hear my voice because you don't know my Word."* At that early stage of my life when I was still a babe in Christ, I came to the conclusion that the Word of God is the voice of God. With this understanding, I began searching the Scriptures (John 5:39). It was there I found the first prophecy of my life which has kept me soaring till this very day.

The LORD shall increase you more and more, you and your children (Ps.115:14, KJV).

From that Scripture, the Holy Spirit told me three things about my future.
- I would be blessed. "***The Lord shall increase you...***"
- The blessing of God on my life would be progressive. "***...more and more...***"
- I would get married we would be blessed with children "***...you and your children,***" And when He talked about my children, my marriage was a surety.

Friends, this is not about memorizing scriptures just so we can check off a box, rather we need to submit ourselves wholly to the words and be personally persuaded enough to engage in all scriptural requirements (activities) that guarantee the fulfillment. It is only on this ground that you can use particular Scriptures as legal evidence against an adversary in spiritual court (warfare).

About five years ago, I relocated to the United States of America. One of my major concerns was what was I supposed to do with the young ministry I was privileged to head. All the human counsel I sought did not seem to be the perfect will of God for me. Then, while praying one day a Scripture sounded in my spirit. *"You did not choose me, but I chose you and appointed you so that you might go and bear fruit—fruit that will last--and so that whatever you ask in my name the Father will give you"* (John 15:16). Through that scripture, the Holy Spirit said to me: "the local assembly (church) is a fruit of your ministry and there are many other fruits. It shall not die but endure." When I shared with a friend what the Holy Spirit told me, he simply asked: "was there any other way the Holy Spirit said it apart from John 15:16?"

"It was exactly that Scripture," I replied.

Today, God has proven Himself faithful and has blessed the ministry by giving us a piece of property and we are nearing completion on our building. In light of this, please don't merely memorize scriptures, personalize them.

2. **Spoken Word or Audible Voice:** Every child of God has

the right to hear the voice of God and prophesy. The apostle Paul said: *"But the one who prophesies speaks to people for their strengthening, encouraging and comfort...I would like every one of you to speak in tongues, but I would rather have you prophesy. The one who prophesies is greater than the one who speaks in tongues...* (1 Cor. 14:3, 5). Please understand that this does not in any way undermine the office of a prophet.

The spoken word is what I call the "thus says the Lord." What God speaks through someone to you or speaks to your spirit directly (though the prophecy may not necessarily begin with, "Thus says the Lord," it is still a "Thus says the Lord). Different people have different ways of expressing what the Holy Spirit impressed on their spirit to pass across; hence, the level of your spiritual maturity and sensitivity determines how receptive you will be.

Most people called into the office of a prophet have the grace to hear from God, with or without prior knowledge of existing and corresponding Scriptures. Yet, everyone is responsible for proving what he or she hears by seeking confirmation from the Scriptures. Sometimes, the person through whom God speaks may not have sufficient knowledge to explain more than what was impressed in his/her spirit. Because of this, going back to them for confirmation or explanation may be misleading in these instances. Also, the person(s) God may use to speak to us may or may not have prior knowledge of our experiences. Further, some people can prophesy without knowing who they are talking to, and some don't even know they are prophesying to, except the recipient who knows that he or she just received a prophecy.

So was my experience some time ago when a Senior in a local university attended one of our services. During my teaching, she heard me prophetically dictate the topic of her thesis to her. She submitted the topic just as she heard it come from me and was approved. I was not an expert in her field of studies and no one in the service knew I prophesied, until she came to testify.

Another day, I was teaching on the vision of our ministry in a message I titled; "Building According to Divine Pattern." All that a woman in the church heard was: "how to make your marriage work." She wrote out all the principles according to my teachings. At the close of service, she came to testify how the message had blessed her life and how she was determined to save her marriage by applying those principles. God always speaks. The question has never been if God will speak, but rather if you (man) will open your heart to hear. *"Remember what it says: 'Today when you hear his voice, don't harden your hearts as Israel did when they rebelled'"* (Heb.3:15 NLT). The method is never the same everywhere at all times. God could speak to someone through another man's testimony. It could be reading of Scripture, preaching of your pastor, prayer, prophetic declaration, or even music.

The unforgettable prophecy that erased all my excuses and dissolved all doubt and questions about my calling as a young believer came through a song ministration. A young girl about 14 years of age ministered in song while I was sitting in the center row in the local church and said, *"I want to use you to fulfill my plan. Before I called you I knew all about you. Oh, my salvation is sure with you in my promise. I have called you; don't complain.* "While the congregation applauded her because of her age and voice, I was in tears because my calling had just been validated and all excuses were erased by that prophetic song. To the glory of God, it's been about 28 years now since that date. Jeremiah 1:5-8 is the corresponding written prophecy that confirmed the prophecy spoken to me in a song. The state of your mind matters. God speaks to us even in songs and in worship. The Scripture confirms this: *"While they were worshiping the Lord and fasting, the Holy Spirit said 'Set apart for me Barnabas and Saul for the work to which I have called them'"* (Acts 13:2).

In my book *When True Love Calls*, there is the testimony of a young lady who had two young men proposing marriage to her at the same time. One was a business man and the other was a school teacher. Subjecting these two men to the same test, the businessman always seems to be a better choice in all ways and areas. Friends and relatives counseled that she should settle for the businessman until one day in church, her pastor was preaching and said, "Don't reject a man because he is a teacher today, he could turn out to be a wealthy man tomorrow."

Every other word that followed as the pastor continued to preach did not concern this lady as her mind had been captured by that powerful and specific saying. According to the testimony, the young lady went to the altar with the teacher, though it was not without persecution from her parents and so-called loved ones.

After about three years of marriage, she had a baby and was pregnant with another one. One day she parked her car to go into a shopping mall when she saw a mad man coming towards her. On a closer look, she discovered he was the businessman she was tempted to marry four years ago.

In tears of gratitude to God, she narrated her testimony to the people who responded to her shout. At this time, the teacher of yesterday had become a wealthy business man as prophetically declared by her pastor. Why be absent from a church service when you don't know when God will speak concerning you and your situation? *"Keep thy foot when thou goest to the house of God, and be more ready to hear, than to give the sacrifice of fools: for they consider not that they do evil"* (Eccl. 5:1).

3. **Dreams and Visions:** A Prophet in the Old Testament was also called a seer. Though this book is a compilation of my teachings, on a certain day a brother came to me and said: "Pastor, thank you for this book, it's really a blessing." When I denied being the author of such a book, he opened it, showed me the contents and said, "all these were your teachings. I was in church when you did all these teachings." I opened my eyes and lo it was a vision. That was a way of God telling me to write this book.

Abraham and Samuel are some of the old prophets who operated in this realm. The prophecy of the Israelite's slavery and deliverance was given to Abraham in a dream.

> *As the sun was setting, Abram fell into a deep sleep,*
> *and a thick and dreadful darkness came over him.*

Then the LORD said to him, "Know for certain that for four hundred years your descendants will be strangers in a country not their own and that they will be enslaved and mistreated there. But I will punish the nation they serve as slaves, and afterward they will come out with great possessions." (Gen.15:12-14)

Samuel's first encounter with God was in a dream.

Now Samuel did not yet know the LORD: The word of the LORD had not yet been revealed to him. A third time the LORD called, "Samuel!" And Samuel got up and went to Eli and said, "Here I am; you called me." Then Eli realized that the LORD was calling the boy. So Eli told Samuel, "Go and lie down, and if he calls you, say, 'Speak, LORD, for your servant is listening.'" So Samuel went and lay down in his place. The LORD came and stood there, calling as at the other times, "Samuel! Samuel!" Then Samuel said, "Speak, for your servant is listening." And the LORD said to Samuel: "See, I am about to do something in Israel that will make the ears of everyone who hears about it tingle." (1 Sam. 3:7-11)

The apostle Peter had a similar encounter in Acts 10:10-19, 28. It reads: "…*While Peter was wondering about the meaning of the vision, the men sent by Cornelius found out where Simon's house was and stopped at the gate. … While Peter was still thinking about the vision, the Spirit said to him, 'Simon, three men are looking for you.'"* Visions and dreams involve seeing images like drama, hearing of voice(s) or being involved in a conversation/actions. Joseph soared into his destiny with the prophecy given him in a dream (*See* Gen. 37:5-11). Any force against you because of the prophecy on your life is helping you without knowing.

While it's expedient to note that dreams could have direct or indirect, open, or hidden meaning (See Gen.40 and 41), it is also of utmost importance to note that no particular dream could be interpreted the same at all times and situations. It could depend on who is involved, the maturity of the person, his/her relationship with the Holy Spirit, the situation/circumstances surrounding it, and perhaps what God is communicating. In as much as many people interpret serpent to mean evil, God could be telling you to be wise (See Matt. 10:19). Eating in the dream does not always mean the same thing. You could simply be hungry, or the particular dream might mean what you wanted is not what you eat, or a correction/rebuke against greed and self-centeredness, or fruits of your labor, or reconciliation. God may be telling you to reconcile with somebody you are holding a grudge against when you exchange food in a dream or eat with the person or when the person is in the picture. The only spiritual beings who gave food to people in the bible were angels. There is no single reference where demons gave anybody food. And according to David in Psalm 23:5, only the Lord prepares a table before His people. Plucking of fruits could mean harvest, soul winning, evangelism prosperity, or fruitfulness. Your understanding of the written word of God could affect your interpretation. Your interpretation determines your application. And your application determines if you will soar or descend.

Remember, when you pray amiss the answer from God is not guaranteed.

To have a definite interpretation to a particular dream at all times and situations is to limit the person and ministry of the Holy Spirit, or a total display of ignorance. The Holy Spirit helps us understand dreams and revelations from God. *"For who among men knows the things of the man, except the spirit of the man within him? So also, no one knows the things of God, except the Spirit of God. Now we have not received the spirit of the world, but the Spirit from God, that we may know the things having been granted to us by God..."* 1 Cor.2:11-12. Spiritual dreams and revelations should not be interpreted with natural knowledge. Things from God need the Spirit of God to interpret and give understanding. **BEWARE!**

✿

4. Word of wisdom and word of knowledge: Word of wisdom is a special gift that enables the prophet to see the far future and the far past while word of knowledge is the ability to see the immediate future and immediate past. Moses, whom the Bible called a great prophet, wrote about the creation through the operation of the gift of the word of wisdom. *"Since then, no prophet has risen in Israel like Moses, whom the LORD knew face to face"* (Deut. 34:10).

 . Any force against you because of the prophecy on your life is helping you without knowing. , **"**

Moses was given a divinely inspired account of what transpired during the first week on earth. Certainly he was not present to witness those events; he looked into the past by his prophetic testimony. On the other hand, when he addresses issues during and after their wilderness experience, he was dealing with immediate conditions.

This gift was also manifested through Solomon.

"For to one is given by the Spirit the word of wisdom; to another the word of knowledge by the same Spirit." (1 Cor. 12:8)

The operation of the gifts of word of wisdom and word of knowledge is similar to the gift of spoken word or audible voice and synonymous with discernment.

5. **Prophetic declaration:** This is totally different from "thus said the Lord," though the operations are very similar. The main difference is while "thus said the Lord" is never a prediction, a prophetic declaration could possibly be a prediction which requires activation of the faith of the hearer. *"Who confirms the word of his servant and fulfills the counsel of his messengers, who says of Jerusalem, 'She shall be inhabited,' and of the cities of Judah, 'They shall be built, and I will raise up their ruins"* (Isa. 44:26). It's the declaration of the inspired, faith-filled written word of God, targeted to address issues for whoever will believe and be willing to meet the scriptural demand for the fulfillment at a particular time. It is a faith declaration banking absolutely on God to honor them. *"Now Elijah the Tishbite, from Tishbe in*

Gilead, said to Ahab, 'As the LORD, the God of Israel, lives, whom I serve, there will be neither dew nor rain in the next few years except at my word'" (1 Kings 17:1).

Faith in your man of God makes the words he speaks into your life wind under your wings that keeps you soaring into your destiny (See 2 Chr. 20:20). Sometimes, it could be directed to you. Another time, you claim it by faith by fulfilling the corresponding obligations, even when it was not primarily directed to you. *"And what I say unto you I say unto all, Watch"* (Mk. 13:37). Faith is what compels you to take corresponding actions to bring the prophetic word of God to fruition in your life.

6. **Observations and circumstances:** Sometimes God uses situations to get your attention. It could be you have failed to heed the inner voice of the Holy Spirit, or you are engrossed in your plans that seem good to your understanding, or God just chose to speak to you through an experience. For example, Jeremiah needed to observe the process of the clay on the potter's wheel so he could understand God's power and authority to fashion man into whatever pleases Him. The voice of God came to Jeremiah after the observations (Jer.18:2-6). If only you could listen and observe, there is always a voice in every experience.

Moses was another man who evaded God's calling for his life. He was so enthralled with keeping Jethro's flock that he dismissed the passion that drove him to murder an Egyptian when he was about 40. God could only get his attention after Moses observed a blazing fire from the middle of a bush that was not consumed (Ex. 3:1-6).

There was a time when I suffered from depression. My mood was completely opposite from who I used to be. Even in church, I could not function or lift my hands in praise to God. I lost my joy, and I could only experience temporal excitement when I was around people. I was fearful, confused, anxious, and prayer was a struggle. To make things worse, I became unproductive in every area. This experience lingered for about 14 months.

Although some people close to me observed the change in my disposition, no one, including myself, could ascertain what the problem was. Then one day, while in a fellowship with co-workers, I was enraptured with a particular brother's dancing steps and his general attitude during praise. Amazed, I said within myself, *I used to dance like this in church, what happened to me?* Immediately the Holy Spirit took me down the memory lane of how it all happened and said: "you have been depressed." As soon as I acknowledged my depression, I became joyful and felt as if a heavy burden had been removed from me. This was how I got freedom from depression. My point is, I needed to see that particular brother express his joy of salvation before I could hear the voice that freed me from depression. Above all, what I know today about the symptoms, manifestations, and how to be free from depression won't be found in psychology books. It was learned from that experience.

God speaks to us through our everyday experiences good or bad. Where God is taking you determines where He will take you through. Observation is beyond the physical. It is seeing with the eyes and hearing with the ears of your spirit. A good observation always leads to positive conclusions. When you go through the fire, water, valley, mountain, divorce, financial hardship, rejection, loss of loved ones, never focus on the situation but focus on the message God is about to communicate to you. Some people may need to experience hardship before they will learn how to manage and multiply what they have, like Isaac who had promises of greatness. If there was no famine, he wouldn't have learned to invent an irrigation system (Gen.26:1-16).

"The voice of the Lord is upon the waters; The God of glory thunders; The Lord is over many waters" (Ps.29:3 AMP). Always bear in mind that nothing just happens to you. Instead, everything happens for your good (Rom. 8:28).

> **Prophecy, either through teaching, preaching, revelation, word of knowledge, or word of wisdom…are for us and our children to do.**

Notes

CHAPTER FOUR

WARRING WITH PROPHECIES

"This charge I entrust to you, Timothy, my child, in accordance with the prophecies previously made about you, that by them you may wage the good warfare" (1Tim.1:18 ESV).

"Set out now and cross the Arnon Gorge. See, I have given into your hand Sihon the Amorite, king of Heshbon, and his country. Begin to take possession of it and engage him in battle" (Deut. 2:24).

Every prophecy of Scripture is for all who believe. There is no prophecy God is not willing or able to fulfill. *"...so is my word that goes out from my mouth: It will not return to me empty, but will accomplish what I desire and achieve the purpose for which I sent it"* (Isa. 55:11). Man's responsibility is to position himself for its fulfillment. Until you are rightly positioned, you may continue missing the target. Be it success or failure, victory or defeat, poverty or prosperity, health or sickness, all have their root in the spirit. *"Beloved, I pray that in every way you may succeed and prosper and be in good health [physically], just as [I know] your soul prospers [spiritually]"* (3 John 1:2 AMP). The level of your spiritual prosperity can either set a pace or set a limitation on the tangibility and physical manifestation of prophecy in your life.

Spiritual warfare existed before the creation of this present earth. Before the earth became empty and void in Gen.1:2, Prophet Isaiah, Jerimiah, and Ezekiel gave different accounts of the warfare that resulted in the emptiness reported by Moses in Genesis 1:2.

> *I looked at the earth, and it was formless and empty; and at the heavens, and their light was gone. I looked at the mountains, and they were quaking; all the hills were swaying. I looked, and there were no people; every bird in the sky had flown away. I looked, and the fruitful land was a desert; all its towns lay in ruins before the LORD, before his fierce anger. This is what the LORD says: "The whole land will be ruined, though I will not destroy it completely."* (Jer.4:23-27 Also see Isa.14:12-17 and Eze.28:12-19)

Despite all that Satan did, God promised not to make a complete end of the earth. Yes, the war for our destiny started when the birth of a Savior was promised by God. *"And I will put enmity between you and the woman, and between your offspring and hers; he will crush your head, and you will strike his heel"* (Gen.3:15). It's imperative we know that every promise or prophecy concerning us will always attract opposition from the devil. Therefore, warfare is you refusing the activities and influence of the opposition in your life. It is a daily, unending and worthy spiritual battle that requires knowledge and adequate preparations or training like David called it. *"A psalm of David. Praise the LORD, who is my rock. He trains my hands for war and gives my fingers skill for battle"* (Ps.144:1).

Knowing that warfare is a daily and unending activity; the need to diligently build walls around your mind is an important step in the quest to win battles in spiritual warfare. Prophecy as a divine declaration of your destination is a legal spiritual weapon that can be deployed against the strategies of the devil.

The word of God is the most reliable, certain, confirmed, sure, true, and firm prophecy and is without human interference. God with His angels always stand to monitor the fulfillment of true prophecy because God knows Satan will always attempt to oppose the fulfillment. *"The LORD said to me, you have seen correctly, for I am watching to see that my word is fulfilled"* (Jer.1:12). *"Take the helmet of salvation and the sword of the Spirit, which is the word of God"* (Eph. 6:17). The Spiritual sword for spiritual battle is the word of God. To be ignorant of what is spoken concerning you is to face your enemies without a sword or weapon.

Prophecies are the evidences that give you confidence in the face of challenges. As you fight in the natural to enforce any will that is beneficial to you, you fight to enforce prophecies because all you will ever be is in it. Fighting in this context encompasses all activities to ensure practical delivery and settlements of all that is settled in heaven concerning you. Warring with prophecies is using the word of God as a standard to determine what you accept, what you reject from your life, and what disqualifies every contrary statement (lies).

Warfare is anything and everything done in the light of God's word to help you become who God says you are. And warfare is fought both in words and in deeds.

The Psalmist puts it in this way; *"May these words of my mouth and this meditation of my heart be pleasing in your sight, LORD, my Rock and my Redeemer"* (Ps.19:4). Through meditation you pray continuously and fight ceaselessly. Praying always in the spirit at all times is made possible through meditation and actions. *"Pray in the Spirit at all times and on every occasion. Stay alert and be persistent in your prayers for all believers everywhere"* (Eph. 6:18).

Meditation make prayer timeless and births corresponding actions. For instance, to adhere to your doctor's prescription is a way to pray for healing by your action. Proper nutrition is a way of praying to be healthy with your action, and to engage your hands is a way to pray for prosperity without the use of words.

WISDOM IN WARFARE:

Warfare is not only about chasing the devil; it is also about the right application of knowledge (wisdom). The greatest enemy of all time and opposition to the fulfillment of prophecies is ignorance. Lack of knowledge is the reason many people live below God's original plan for their lives.

The Scripture says; *"My people are destroyed from lack of knowledge. Because you have rejected knowledge, I also reject you as my priests; because you have ignored the law of your God, I also will ignore your children"* (Hosea 4:6). To be destroyed in this context is to be stripped of power, honor, and glory. It is to be made lower than one's original position. God said, the problem of my people is not that demons have multiplied or Satan has gained more power, but that they lack and reject knowledge. The warfare against ignorance is not prayer but to seek knowledge. Ignorance is the greatest opposition to destiny, and knowledge is the greatest opposition to ignorance. Therefore, every opportunity to acquire knowledge is an opportunity to be equipped with weapons against ignorance.

But knowledge alone cannot set any man free unless this knowledge is rightly applied. The right application of knowledge is wisdom. That is why the best prayer, even in warfare is, "Lord, what do you want me to do?" (See Acts 22:10)

So what is wisdom?

First, wisdom is knowing what to do and doing it: *"Anyone who listens to my teaching and follows it is **wise**, like a person who builds a house on solid rock. Though the rain comes in torrents and the floodwaters rise and the winds beat against that house, it won't collapse because it is built on bedrock. But anyone who hears my teaching and doesn't obey it is **foolish**, like a person who builds a house on sand. When the rains and floods come and the winds beat against that house, it will collapse with a mighty crash"* (Matt. 7:24-27).

Second, wisdom is doing the word of God: *"For wisdom is a protection even as money is a protection, But the [excellent] advantage of knowledge is that wisdom shields and preserves the lives of its possessors"* (Eccl. 7:12). From this passage, we can see that wisdom is both an offensive and defensive weapon. Therefore, in addition to prayer, a wise warfare strategy is to commit all requirements towards fulfillment of prophecy.

"Beloved, I pray that in every way you may succeed and prosper and be in good health [physically], just as [I know] your soul prospers [spiritually]." (3 John 1:2 AMP)

Your prosperity and healthy living tops God's priority. However, you must fulfill some basic principles of prosperity if you want the tangible to be experienced. The commitment to these principles is wisdom, which is a weapon of warfare.

WORK: Just as work is a warfare strategy against poverty, idleness is the enemy's strategy against your success. *"That person is like a tree planted by streams of water, which yields its fruit in season and whose leaf does not wither-- whatever they do prospers"* (Ps. 1:3). This was the testimony of Joseph: He prospered in all that he did. *"...Now his master saw that the LORD was with him and how the LORD caused all that he did to prosper in his hand..."* (Gen. 39:2-5). Joseph prospered as a slave, a prisoner, and a prime minister. So never forget that *"Idle hands make one poor, but diligent hands bring riches"* (Prov. 10:4 and 22:29).

MANAGEMENT SKILLS: Many are poor not because they lack resources but because they lack the ability to manage what is available. Divine resource flows in the direction of good managers. The Scripture declares that God did not send rain to the earth until He found a manager. *"For the LORD God had not yet sent rain to water the earth, and there were no* *people to cultivate the soil"* (Gen. 2:5). If you can manage little, God will give you much. *"If you are faithful in little things, you will be faithful in large ones. But if you are dishonest in little things, you won't be honest with greater responsibilities"* (Luke 16:10).

Accountability is a principle of management and stewardship (tithing) is a proof of accountability. When you give your stewardship according to the Scriptures, you validate your management ability, register for more, and when your obedience is complete, God will avenge every disobedience that may oppose your increase and comfort. Your total compliance with God's word is fundamental.

> **❝**When you give your stewardship according to the Scriptures, you validate your management ability, register for more, and when your obedience is complete... **❞**

Generally, giving is a warfare strategy against poverty and lack. Ignorance of the law of sowing and reaping could render prosperity prophecy unfulfilled. *"As long as the earth endures, seedtime and harvest, cold and heat, summer and winter, day and night will never cease"* (Gen. 8:22). The prophecy of prosperity and others will be fulfilled by the right applications of knowledge. That is why Satan's most effective strategy is ignorance. *"Satan, who is the god of this world, has blinded the minds of those who don't believe. They are unable to see the glorious light of the Good News. They don't understand this message about the glory of Christ, who is the exact likeness of God"* (2 Cor. 4:4 NLT).

Of course, we saw that not only does God want us to prosper, He also wants us to be healthy. Now, there are basic principles to be practiced if you must be in health:

1. **GOOD EATING HABITS**: Never eat because of taste; eat because of your health. To seek the satisfaction of your tongue may be detrimental to your entire body system. Everything helpful to your body can also be harmful when eaten wrongly or in excess. Even water, which is necessary for life, can kill if too much is drank at once. So, you should not eat every food. *"And put a knife to your throat if you are a man of great appetite"* (**Prov.23:2**).

Abstain from fattening food and things with high cholesterol (See Deut. 14:8 and Dan. 1:12, 15). Eat more foods that grow on trees and plants and cut back on food manufactured in plants. And don't forget that fasting is good for healthy living.

According to a recent report published in The Lancet Medical Journal: "No amount of alcohol is good for your overall health." The widely held view of health benefits from alcohol needs revising. While the majority of national guidelines suggest that one or two glasses of wine or beer per day are safe, the report's authors said, "Our result show that the safest level of drinking is none." Regardless of what we may have been told previously and what we are used to, facts are stubborn things.

The study, which was carried out by researchers at the

Institute of Health Metrics and Evaluation in Seattle looked at alcohol use and its health effects on those aged 15 and 95 in 195 countries between 1990 and 2016. It found that alcohol led to 2.8 million deaths in 2016 and was the leading risk factor for premature death and disability among those 15 to 49, accounting for 10 percent of all deaths. Those deaths include alcohol-related cancer and cardiovascular diseases, infectious diseases such as tuberculosis, intentional injuries such as violence and self-harm, traffic accidents and other unintentional injuries such as drowning and fires. Meanwhile, for those over 50, the biggest killer was cancer, particularly among women.

Also, according to American Lung Association: "Smoking harms nearly every organ in the body and is a main cause of lung cancer and chronic obstructive pulmonary disease (COPD). It's also the cause of coronary heart disease, stroke and a host of others." Records shows that smoking related diseases claim more 480,000 American lives each year. Cigarette smoking is the number one cause of preventable disease and death worldwide.

2. **BODILY EXERCISE:** "...*physical exercise has some value*" (1 Tim. 4:8). The little profit in physical exercise could be of great value, and sometimes it may be all your body needs to stay healthy. Getting the appropriate amount of exercise benefits nearly every aspect of a person's health. Not only does exercise help control weight, it also improves mental health, mood, chances of living longer, and the strength of your bones and muscles.

3. **OBSERVE REST TIME:** Resting time is refreshing time. *"By the seventh day God completed His work which He had done, and He rested on the seventh day from all His work which He had done. Then God blessed the seventh day and sanctified it, because in it He rested from all His work which God had created"* (Gen.2:2-3).

Your body needs adequate relaxation to remain healthy. Getting the correct amount of quality sleep is essential to your ability to learn and process memories. Additionally, sleep helps restore your body's energy, repair muscle tissue, and triggers the release of hormones that affect growth and appetite. Recent studies show that; *Relaxation is an important part of maintaining health and wellbeing, and being able to calmly deal with life's stresses. It improves your mental health and gives the body a chance to take a break, releasing muscle tension (that you may not even be aware of), lower blood pressure, improve digestion (the body diverts its focus back to digestion and other maintenance and repair processes instead of being in an alert/alarm phase. Massage, exercise, meditation, reading books, craftwork, sleeping are all methods of achieving relaxation. Choose something that you enjoy, that gives you a sense of satisfaction and that you feel best relaxes both your body and mind.*

4. **ENGAGE IN KINGDOM SERVICE:** *"You must serve only the LORD your God. If you do, I will bless you with food and water, and I will protect you from illness..."* (Ex. 23:25-6). When you commit yourself to serving the Lord, God will commit Himself to your total well-being and ensure diseases

never distract you from rendering service to Him. Service is a great weapon of warfare. Service is committing your body, energy, time, talents, and resources to the advancement of God's kingdom. It is taking responsibility to ensure the advancement of God's Kingdom. When you serve the Lord, the Lord will service you.

5. **SEXUAL DISCIPLINE:** Sex is both spiritual and physical. There is always a transfer of spirit in the same way diseases are transmitted between sex partners. Sexual discipline will free you from diseases that are only transmitted through sex (1 Cor. 6:18-20).

To fulfill the prophecies of marital bliss, the principle of Unconditional Love, Submission, Forgiveness, Tolerance, Knowledge, and Patience... must be strictly adhered to. Also, a student who desires to fulfill the prophecy of maintaining the top only, and not below, must be diligent in his studies. *"...No, I worked harder than all of them--yet not I, but the grace of God that was with me"* (1 Cor.15:10).

All these are uncommon warfare strategies. Though not necessarily listed as weapons of spiritual warfare, this is wisdom that makes spiritual warfare productive.

To punish disobedience, you must first complete your obedience. *And we will be ready to punish every act of disobedience, once your obedience is complete* (2 Cor.10:6). You can only exercise authority when you live under authority. Obedience to the word of God puts you under the authority of

God, and in return, makes you an authority over your situation. *"The centurion replied, 'Lord, I do not deserve to have you come under my roof. But just say the word, and my servant will be healed. For I myself am a man under authority, with soldiers under me. I tell this one, 'Go,' and he goes; and that one, 'Come,' and he comes. I say to my servant, 'Do this,' and he does it....'"* (Matt. 8:8-9). Putting yourself under subjection puts you in authority over the forces that want to negate God's word for your life.

Consequently, warring with prophecies is praying or engaging in activities with full focus of what God said concerning you. That means, when you exercise, you do so with the consciousness to enforce the prophecy of divine health. The same is true of eating. You eat with wisdom and command what you eat to nourish your body. *"And whatever you do, whether in word or deed, do it all in the name of the Lord Jesus, giving thanks to God the Father through him"* (Col. 3:17).

6. **THE PLACE OF PRAYER**: Prayer in this context of warfare is saying no to thoughts, imaginations, suggestions, and oppositions to the prophecies on your life. Warring with prophecies is refusing to give up in the face of any opposition and challenge. It's laying claim on the word with determination to see it manifest in your life. It is saying "yes" and "amen" in word and in deeds.

In prayer, you verbally or meditatively declare the word of God against any mountain, exercise the authority in the name of Jesus against satanic operations and every set-up of the enemy to hinder the fulfillment of God's word concerning you. When you constantly declare the prophecy on your life your faith will be stirred, your focus will be enhanced, and hope will come alive. *"Don't worry about anything; instead, pray about everything. Tell God what you need, and thank him for all he has done."* (Phil. 4:6). Through prayer you use the hammer of God's word to break every stone; you use the fire of God's word to melt every Iron Gate against your destiny; and you assign your ministry angels for performance. Through prayer you align yourself and your words with God's; receive power from God to change the things you need to change; receive light, directions, the courage to walk through the mountains that may never move, and go through every valley without fear. The essence of warfare is to defy anything capable of hindering you from reaching your destination (which is the prophecy). Through prayer you constantly remind God of His promises (prophecies).

WINNING ATTITUDE: *"Then Caleb silenced the people before Moses and said, 'We should go up and take possession of the land, for we can certainly do it'* (Num.13:30). Be prepared to go up at once and take control, because you can definitely conquer. God's word will never return to Him unfulfilled. **Be Wise and Rise**.

When you constantly declare the prophecy on your life your faith will be stirred, your focus will be enhanced, and hope will come alive.

Notes

CHAPTER FIVE

PROPHETIC AGENDA

"You will hear of wars and rumors of wars, but see to it that you are not alarmed. Such things must happen, but the end is still to come." (Matt. 24:6)

Prophetic agendas are God's programs of events that must happen with time. No man can pray against it. You can only seek to be exempted. As the glory of the Lord is coming upon the church of Jesus Christ in a very heavy manner, gross darkness will take over the earth. The world will seek answers to their questions and solutions to their problems from the church. The wisdom of this world shall fail. If you are a true believer, arise, for your time of glory has come.

Here are some scriptures on God's prophetic agenda that I'd like you to ponder:

1. *Arise, shine, for your light has come, and the glory of the Lord rises upon you. See, darkness covers the earth and thick darkness is over the peoples, but the Lord rises upon you and his glory appears over you. Nations will come to your light, and kings to the brightness of your dawn. Lift up your eyes and look about you: All assemble and come to you; your sons come from afar, and your daughters are carried on the hip. Then you will look and be radiant, your heart will throb and swell with joy; the wealth on the*

seas will be brought to you, to you the riches of the nations will come. Herds of camels will cover your land, young camels of Midian and Ephah. And all from Sheba will come, bearing gold and incense and proclaiming the praise of the Lord. All Kedar's flocks will be gathered to you, the rams of Nebaioth will serve you; they will be accepted as offerings on my altar, and I will adorn my glorious temple. Who are these that fly along like clouds, like doves to their nests? Surely the islands look to me; in the lead are the ships of Tarshish, bringing your children from afar, with their silver and gold, to the honor of the Lord your God, the Holy One of Israel, for he has endowed you with splendor. Foreigners will rebuild your walls, and their kings will serve you. Though in anger I struck you, in favor I will show you compassion. Your gates will always stand open, they will never be shut, day or night, so that people may bring you the wealth of the nations- their kings led in triumphal procession. For the nation or kingdom that will not serve you will perish; it will be utterly ruined. The glory of Lebanon will come to you, the juniper, the fir and the cypress together, to adorn my sanctuary; and I will glorify the place for my feet. The children of your oppressors will come bowing before you; all who despise you will bow down at your feet and will call you the City of the Lord, Zion of the Holy One of Israel. (Isa.60:1-14)

2. *Jesus answered: "Watch out that no one deceives you. For many will come in my name, claiming, 'I am the Messiah,' and will deceive many. You will hear of wars and rumors of wars, but see to it that you are not alarmed. Such things must happen, but the end is still to come. Nation will rise against nation, and kingdom against kingdom. There will be famines and earthquakes in various places. All these are the beginning of birth pains.*

"Then you will be handed over to be persecuted and put to

death, and you will be hated by all nations because of me. At that time many will turn away from the faith and will betray and hate each other, and many false prophets will appear and deceive many people. Because of the increase of wickedness, the love of most will grow cold, but the one who stands firm to the end will be saved. And this gospel of the kingdom will be preached in the whole world as a testimony to all nations, and then the end will come. "So when you see standing in the holy place 'the abomination that causes desolation,' spoken of through the prophet Daniel—let the reader understand— then let those who are in Judea flee to the mountains. Let no one on the housetop go down to take anything out of the house. Let no one in the field go back to get their cloak. How dreadful it will be in those days for pregnant women and nursing mothers! Pray that your flight will not take place in winter or on the Sabbath. For then there will be great distress, unequaled from the beginning of the world until now—and never to be equaled again. "If those days had not been cut short, no one would survive, but for the sake of the elect those days will be shortened. At that time if anyone says to you, 'Look, here is the Messiah!' or, 'There he is!' do not believe it. For false messiahs and false prophets will appear and perform great signs and wonders to deceive, if possible, even the elect. See, I have told you ahead of time. "So if anyone tells you, 'There he is, out in the wilderness,' do not go out; or, 'Here he is, in the inner rooms,' do not believe it. For as lightning that comes from the east is visible even in the west, so will be the coming of the Son of Man. Wherever there is a carcass, there the vultures will gather.

"Immediately after the distress of those days "'the sun will be darkened, and the moon will not give its light; the stars will fall from the sky, and the heavenly bodies will be shaken.' "Then will appear the sign of the Son of Man in heaven. And then all the

peoples of the earth will mourn when they see the Son of Man coming on the clouds of heaven, with power and great glory. And he will send his angels with a loud trumpet call, and they will gather his elect from the four winds, from one end of the heavens to the other. "Now learn this lesson from the fig tree: As soon as its twigs get tender and its leaves come out, you know that summer is near. Even so, when you see all these things, you know that it is near, right at the door. Truly I tell you, this generation will certainly not pass away until all these things have happened. Heaven and earth will pass away, but my words will never pass away." (Matt.24: 4-35)

3. *"I will drive the northern horde far from you, pushing it into a parched and barren land; its eastern ranks will drown in the Dead Sea and its western ranks in the Mediterranean Sea. And its stench will go up; its smell will rise. "Surely he has done great things! Do not be afraid, land of Judah be glad and rejoice. Surely the Lord has done great things! Do not be afraid, you wild animals, for the pastures in the wilderness are becoming green. The trees are bearing their fruit; the fig tree and the vine yield their riches. Be glad, people of Zion, rejoice in the Lord your God, for he has given you the autumn rain because he is faithful. He sends you abundant showers, both autumn and spring rains, as before. The threshing floors will be filled with grain; the vats will overflow with new wine and oil. "I will repay you for the years the locusts have eaten the great locust and the young locust, the other locusts and the locust swarm my great army that I sent among you. You will have plenty to eat, until you are full, and you will praise the name of the Lord your God, who has worked wonders for you; never again will my people be shamed. Then you will know that I am in Israel that*

I am the Lord your God, and that there is no other; never again will my people be shamed. "And afterward, I will pour out my Spirit on all people. Your sons and daughters will prophesy, your old men will dream dreams, your young men will see visions. Even on my servants, both men and women, I will pour out my Spirit in those days. I will show wonders in the heavens and on the earth blood and fire and billows of smoke. The sun will be turned to darkness and the moon to blood before the coming of the great and dreadful day of the Lord. And everyone who calls on the name of the Lord will be saved; for on Mount Zion and in Jerusalem there will be deliverance as the Lord has said, even among the survivors whom the Lord calls. (Joel 2:20-32)

There are uncountable prophetic agendas in the Scripture. Some have happened, some are happening already, and many are yet to happen. Understanding of these events that are certain to happen prepares you, and your faith in prophecies puts wind under your wings to soar while many others are descending. The joy of knowing what the future holds through the Scripture is enough to keep one soaring amidst the storms of life. The Scripture is the picture of your future.

Now you know there will be a time when others will (experience a casting down) say there is a casting down, you better prepare to (experience a lifting up) say there is a lifting up. Everybody may be faced with the same situations; but your responses to the situations will make a difference. The storm that brings down other birds is the same storm that helps the eagle attain her highest heights. The flood that destroyed the earth was the same flood that lifted the ark of Noah. The famine that turned many into slaves, is the same famine that

> **"** . .
> The Scripture is
> the picture of
> your future. ,
> **"**

turned Joseph into Prime Minister. But remember, as a believer you carry the mark of exemption. Because of the mark of the blood, every evil will certainly pass you and your household over. For this reason, do not call conspiracy everything this people calls a conspiracy; do not fear what they fear, and do not dread it (Isa. 8:12).

But now, this is what the LORD says-- he who created you, Jacob, he who formed you, Israel: "Do not fear, for I have redeemed you; I have summoned you by name; you are mine. When you pass through the waters, I will be with you; and when you pass through the rivers, they will not sweep over you. When you walk through the fire, you will not be burned; the flames will not set you ablaze. For I am the LORD your God, the Holy One of Israel, your Savior; I give Egypt for your ransom, Cush and Seba in your stead. Since you are precious and honored in my sight, and because I love you, I will give people in exchange for you, nations in exchange for your life. Do not be afraid, for I am with you; I will bring your children from the east and gather you from the west. I will say to the north, "Give them up!' and to the south, Do not hold them back. Bring my sons from afar and my daughters from the ends of the earth" (Isa. 43:1-6). Hallelujah!

Prophecies will never return to God unfulfilled. *"As the rain and the snow come down from heaven, and do not return to it without watering the earth and making it bud and flourish, so that it yields seed for the sower and bread for the eater, so is my word that goes out from my mouth: It will not return to me empty, but will accomplish what I desire and achieve the purpose for which I sent it"* (Isa.55:10-11).

"Heaven and earth will pass away, but my words will never pass away." (Matt. 24:35)

God knows you by name. There is a miracle with your name on it. You are God's. You will not miss your place in destiny. His presence will always abide with you. You must finish well with testimonies in your mouth and a new song in your tongue. You will not faint before your due season. You will not see shame. The glory of the Lord will be seen upon you. You must shine in the midst of darkness. You will be a leader of nations. You will not experience less than God's word concerning you. This water will not drown you, but will clean you up. You will not be burnt in this fire, it will purify you and make you come out as gold. Yes, your ending shall be better than the beginning. God will bring you into the company of people who will value and celebrate your uniqueness and gifting. You will soar above this storm. You will not be small; the Lord will make your name great. In the name of Jesus, Amen.

And so shall it be because the Lord says so.
HALLELUJAH!
Keep soaring to higher heights.

> **God will bring you into the company of people who will value and celebrate your uniqueness and gifting**

📋 *Notes*

_____

_____

_____

_____

_____

_____

_____

_____

_____

_____

CHAPTER SIX

FAITH IS A MUST

"And without faith it is impossible to please God, because anyone who comes to him must believe that he exists and that he rewards those who earnestly seek him." (Heb. 11:6)

There are few things that are "musts" in the Scripture. Prophetic agenda is one of them (See Matt. 24:6). Being born again is another one. It is a must for whoever wants to see the kingdom of God (See John 3:7). True worshipers must worship in spirit and in truth (John 4:24). And Faith is also a must.

Faith is compulsory. It's not optional; neither is it just for some people. It is a must for all who are and will have a relationship with God. As it is impossible to see the kingdom of God without being born again, so it is impossible to please God without faith. What physical breathing is to our physical existence, so is faith to our spiritual existence. As you must breath to live, so you must have faith to have and keep a relationship with God. *"Then Jesus said, 'Did I not tell you that if you believe, you will see the glory of God?'"* (John 11:40). Absolute confidence in God and His word is what brings the manifestation of the prophecy.

Faith is what attracts God's attention to man. *"I tell you, he will see that they get justice, and quickly. However, when the Son of*

Man comes, will he find faith on the earth?" (Luke 18:8). And faith is what the devil, our enemy, seeks to attack. *"But I have prayed for you, Simon, that your faith may not fail. And when you have turned back, strengthen your brothers"* (Luke 22:32). God blesses you when He finds faith in you, and is helpless when and where there is no faith.

It is clear from the Scripture that absolute faith in God is never static but active. For the Scripture says; *"For as the body without the spirit is dead, so faith without works is dead also"* (James 2:17-26). Faith without works is a dead faith; because the lack of works reveals an unchanged life or a spiritually dead heart. In others words, the proof that you believe in God is seen in what you do towards fulfilling the prophecy in your life.

God is grieved when we doubt His integrity. This is one of the reasons Satan opposes and delays the fulfillment of God's word so as to make us doubt God. But when your faith in God is absolute, results becomes inevitable.

The Scripture in Romans 4: 20-21 said this concerning Abraham, *"He did not waver in unbelief at God's promise but was strengthened in his faith and gave glory to God, because he was fully convinced that what He had promised He was also able to perform."* Faith in God is the force that compels the believer to perform. Unbelief on the other hand means you don't trust God enough to keep His promise. But Abraham was different; he was persuaded of God's ability and willingness to perform His promise regardless of the age of him and his wife.

God is hurt when you can't trust Him to the end. Every act of unbelief means you are putting God in the same class as men who cannot own up to their word. But absolute faith means endless possibilities. "*'If you can?' said Jesus. 'Everything is possible for one who believes'*" (Mark 9:23). Again, the Scripture says, "*Jesus looked at them and said, 'With man this is impossible, but with God all things are possible'*" (Matt. 19:26). That means when you believe, God infuses you with His ability to act in His class of all-around possibilities. Our God is a generous God. When you believe Him, He shares His ability to make all things possible with you. He brings you to His class and causes you to do what only He can do.

Faith is for doing. Faith is for work. Faith is the work that makes things work. Anything working has been worked by faith, and whatever is not working has not been worked. In the same way you work out your salvation, according to Apostle Paul "*...continue to work out your salvation with fear and trembling*" (Phil.2:12), so also you work out all prophecies and promises of God by continuous obedience and with deep reverence.

Anything left to itself belongs to the devil. This is in accordance with Sir Isaac Newton's proposition which corresponds with scriptures. It states: *every object will remain at rest or in uniform motion in a straight line unless compelled to change its state by the action of an external force.* But "*If clouds are full of water, they pour rain on the earth. Whether a tree falls to the south or to the north, in the place where it falls, there it will lie*" (Eccl.11:3). Faith in God is the relevant force that turns things around.

If "when a man's ways please the LORD, he makes even his enemies to be at peace with him" (Prov.16:17), and it is impossible to please God without faith (Heb.11:6), it means that faith is what a man needs to silence all his enemies and oppositions of his destiny (prophecy). If I may paraphrase these two verses, "when a man has faith, his enemies will be at peace with him. Faith enables a mortal man to satisfy the divine God. As faith pleases God, unbelief displeases Him.

PARTNERS OF FAITH

The force of faith is powerful, but without its close associates it may not produce the desired result. Some of these associates are Hope and Patience. Now, let us look at these two faith associates in a moment.

HOPE: Hope or expectation is needed for faith to come alive. Where there is no hope, faith cannot be born because faith only presents evidence of what you hope for. *"Faith is the confidence that what we hope for will actually happen; it gives us assurance about things we cannot see"* (Heb. 11:1). When hope is high, faith is strong. When hope is low, faith will be weak. And when hope is dead, faith is buried. That is why you can't have faith in hopelessness. There is no future where there is no hope. Life ends where hope ends. This is why God said His good plan for you is to give you what you hope for. *"'For I know the plans I have for you,' declares the LORD, 'plans to prosper you and not to harm you, plans to give you hope and a future'"* (Jer.29:11).

Thus, a hopeless situation is a helpless situation. And faith, which comes by hearing, only comes to where her close friend, hope, lives. Hope gives invitation to faith. A man can live without food for forty days, water for four days, oxygen four minutes, and hope four seconds. Hope is the root that connects a tree to water while faith is the branches that bear the fruits. The Scripture says; *"At least there is hope for a tree: If it is cut down, it will sprout again, and its new shoots will not fail. Its roots may grow old in the ground and its stump die in the soil, yet at the scent of water it will bud and put forth shoots like a plant"* (Job 14:7-9). Faith is the evidence of hope, as work is the evidence of faith. You have faith because you first have hope.

Again, discouragement and sadness of heart is evidence your hope is disconnected from God. *"Why am I discouraged? Why is my heart so sad? I will put my hope in God! I will praise him again--my Savior and my God"* (Ps. 43:5). But praise brings your hope alive and connects it with God.

PATIENCE: The lack of patience is the only reason faith fails. When faith is tested, it produces patience to keep hope alive (See James 1:3). Faith can only persist as long as there is patience. Patience keeps faith active when hope is delayed. Patience is not just waiting: it's being persistent in well-doing in hope of reaping in due season. Just as faith is trusting God's ability, patience is trusting God's timing. **"God makes everything happen at the right time..."** (Eccl. 3:11 CEV).

Patience is a major prescription for whoever wants to see the fulfillment of what is promised or prophesied. *"Patient endurance is what you need now, so that you will continue to do God's will. Then you will receive all that he has promised"* (Heb. 10:36). When patience is absent it is possible to do the will of God and not receive the promise. This is because faith

> **"**Thus, a hopeless situation is a helpless situation. And faith, which comes by hearing, only comes to where her close friend, hope, lives. Hope gives invitation to faith. **"**

73

makes you please God, while patience makes you wait for the reward of pleasing God. Patience sees ahead of faith. When faith sees the end of the road, patience sees a "T" junction and tells faith to keep going. You need patience because your time and calendar differ from God's. *"A thousand years in your sight are like a day that has just gone by, or like a watch in the night"* (Ps. 90:4). Every prophecy has a set time for its fulfillment. So you are to wait for the set time like Abraham waited for twenty-five years before the promised child was born.

Joseph waited for thirteen years to see his dream fulfilled. David waited for seven years before he was crowned king. And the disciples waited for fifty days to receive the promise of the Holy Spirit. Waiting time is not wasted time. Waiting time is processing time. And when the process is incomplete, the product will be missed. *"We do not want you to become lazy, but to imitate those who through faith and patience inherit what has been promised"* (Heb. 6:12). Patience in the process makes faith in the promises rewarding.

Faith needs hope to come alive and it needs patience to stay alive. So do not give up in doing what is good. Patiently wait for everything you have commanded by faith. The prophecy must come to pass. *"Know also that wisdom is like honey for you: If you find it, there is a future hope for you, and your hope will not be cut off"* (Prov. 24:14). Faith, hope, and patience are invisible forces that produce visible results and makes the impossible possible.

> Nobody regret being patient!
> Many only regret giving up so soon.

📋 *Notes*

> **Faith needs hope to come alive and it needs patience to stay alive. So do not give up in doing what is good.**

Notes

CHAPTER SEVEN

TAKE THE AIR WAYS

"There are three things that are too amazing for me, four that I do not understand: **the way of an eagle in the sky**, *the way of a snake on a rock, the way of a ship on the high seas, and the way of a man with a young woman"* (Prov. 30:18-19).

Mr. Ague, who is considered to be the author of the thirtieth chapter of the book of proverbs, deserves some credit for his excellent observation which resulted in this profound statement. He was serious and careful enough to observe a mystery that resides in four common everyday sights.

The way of an eagle in the air is one of the most amazing and difficult things to understand according to the author of Proverbs 30. Is this not the reality of any man born of the Spirit whose way is a mystery? *"The wind blows wherever it pleases. You hear its sound, but you cannot tell where it comes from or where it is going. So it is with everyone born of the Spirit"* (John 3:8).

Air, though not seen nor always felt, is constantly in motion. It is moving in great circles because of differences in pressure. It drops down in great downdrafts, sometimes because of the contours of the ground beneath and other times due to the effect of the sun and the oceans. There are huge updrafts where warm air rises at very high speeds. The air changes from hour to hour. This huge sea of air, moving in three dimensions, is where the eagle lives.

Somehow the eagle can see or sense all these. He uses the currents of air to support himself and soars with it. He can rise thousands of feet into the air without the slightest effort. He can look around and somehow see air currents moving in the direction he wants to go and lets them carry him along. He doesn't have to flap like a sparrow or most other birds.

And do you know that an eagle can detect when a storm is approaching long before it breaks? Do you know the eagle doesn't hide from the storm? Do you know the worse the storm the higher the eagle goes? It will actually fly to a high spot and wait for the winds to come. When the storm hits, it sets its wings so that the wind will pick it up and lift it above the storm. Isn't that remarkable? While the storm rages below, the eagle is soaring above the tempest below. It does not escape the storm, it simply uses the storm to lift it higher. It rises on the winds that bring the storm. What an extraordinary way to deal with adversity!

There is a wonderful lesson for God's children to learn from the way an eagle approaches a storm. When the storms of life come upon us, we too can rise above them. We can lift ourselves above adversity by setting our minds and hearts toward God and His word of prophecy. The storms do not have to overcome us any more than they can overcome the eagle. We can allow the power of God's word to lift us above them.

> **"** It's therefore wise to take our eyes off the storm, which could just be a process and focus on the promise. **"**

In the midst of life's storms, David said: *"Even though I walk through the valley of the shadow of death, I fear no evil, for You are with me; Your rod and Your staff, they comfort me"* (Ps.23:4). David knew the storm (darkest valley) is a walk-through process and that it's never the destination, but the prophecy (word of God) is. David also understood that the storm could be our passage to greater glory, just as the storm helps the eagle soar high. Remember the word of prophecy Jesus gave to the sisters (Mary and Martha) of Lazarus, when it was reported he was sick: *"When he heard this, Jesus said, 'This sickness will not end in death. No, it is for God's glory so that God's Son may be glorified through it"* (John 11:4). The storm of life, marriage, finance, ministry, and career may go through death, but it will surely end in glory. The process notwithstanding, the glory is your destination.

Furthermore, the storms (or trials) of life can actually help us in our walk of faith. This is because they build something in us that will be a part of our lives forever. Remember what Paul wrote to the congregation at Corinth. *"For our light affliction, which is but for a moment, is working for us a far more exceeding and eternal weight of glory"* (2 Cor. 4:17). What great news to know that the storm of life is actually working something better for us. It's therefore wise to take our eyes off the storm, which could just be a process and focus on the promise. That is, the weight of glory. *"Yet what we suffer now is nothing compared to the glory he will reveal to us later"* (Rom. 8:18). Our God is always intentional.

Here is another thing to meditate on: When the eagle flies above the storm, she is in a sense overcoming it. But she does so in a most interesting way. She capitalized on the strength of the storm, which wanted to destroy her, to rise above it.

> **"** Prophecy may not calm the storm but it is sure to give us peace in the midst of the storm; wisdom to take advantage; and strength to soar higher. **"**

That should also be a great lesson from this book. God wants us to learn how to use our pains for gain. We can use adversity for advantage. The trials we overcome today will become our testimonies tomorrow. And the word of our testimony is the weapon to overcome the devil himself (See Rev. 12:11). Just don't focus on the problem, focus on the promise. We need to learn from trials to grow from the experience and be made better (See James 1:2-3). Sometimes the way of God to the other (better) side of our life, ministry, career, marriage, or finances could be through the valley or through the storm. God, who will not allow trials that are more than we can bear to come our way, could also make a way for us to "escape" trials so we can endure them and be a testimonial to others who may need to go through the same route (See 1 Cor. 10:13). At other times, we should (soar) "flee" to a different position and location (perhaps better and higher) (Matt. 10:23).

Prophecy may not calm the storm but it is sure to give us peace in the midst of the storm; wisdom to take advantage; and strength to soar higher. This was why Jesus could comfortably sleep in the boat even when it seemed the end had come:

> *But soon a fierce storm came up. High waves were breaking into the boat, and it began to fill with water. Jesus was sleeping at the back of the boat with his head on a cushion. The disciples woke him up, shouting, "Teacher, don't you care that we're going to drown?" When Jesus woke up, he rebuked the wind and said to the waves, "Silence! Be still!" Suddenly the wind stopped, and there was a great calm. Then he asked them, "Why are you afraid? Do you still have no faith?" The disciples were absolutely terrified. "Who is this man?" they asked each other. "Even the wind and waves obey him!"*
> (Mark.4:37-41)

Friends, never fear. Only believe. When Jesus said it's time to go over to the other side, the other side is settled. Like the eagle uses the wind to attain her heights, your present storm could be a clue to where God is taking you in life. If you position yourself rightly, you will find testimonies in the trials and message in the mess. The height of the eagle is determined by the strength of the storm. *"Praise be to the God and Father of our Lord Jesus Christ, the Father of compassion and the God of all comfort, who comforts us in all our troubles, so that we can comfort those in any trouble with the comfort we ourselves receive from God"* (2 Cor. 1:3-4). You are not just there for yourself only, but also for many who will

> **❝ You are not just there for yourself only, but also for many who will come after you. ❞**

come after you.   Keep soaring by faith. Keep soaring by the word of God, which is the most reliable prophecy. As the eagle is exceptional among other birds, so will you also be exceptional.

Therefore; TAKE YOUR AIRWAYS AND KEEP SOARING WITH PROPHECIES ABOVE EVERY STORM. See you on the other side.

The storm that brings down other birds is the same storm that helps the eagle attain her highest heights. The flood that destroyed the earth was the same flood that lifted the ark of Noah. But remember, as a believer you carry the mark of exemption. Because of the mark of the blood, every evil will certainly pass you and your household over.

📋 *Notes*

Every prophecy or promise from God, when understood, motivates a person to give glory to God. Even when the prophecy was delayed, Abraham kept praising God. Abraham knew that God values praise because it's one thing God can't do for Himself.

Notes

CHAPTER EIGHT

FOLLOW THE EXAMPLE

"Such things were written in the Scriptures long ago to teach us. And the Scriptures give us hope and encouragement as we wait patiently for God's promises to be fulfilled."
(Rom.15:4 NLT)

"And don't grumble as some of them did, and then were destroyed by the angel of death. These things happened to them as examples for us. They were written down to warn us who live at the end of the age" (1 Cor. 10:10-11 NLT).

The best way parents can correct and instill discipline is by example. The best way leaders lead is by example. And the best way teachers impart knowledge is by example. Inspiring accuracy, excellence, correctness, and averting waste (of time, energy, resources...), is the essence of setting examples. Examples are to be followed if they are good; and not followed, if they are bad. By definition, "example is a thing characteristic of its kind or illustrating a **general rule.** It serves as a pattern to be imitated or not to be imitated."

> **"** The best way leaders lead is by example. And the best way teachers impart knowledge is by example.. **"**

A general rule is a principle that has no geographical

> **"** If what is said to one cannot be said to all, what is said to one should not be said at all.... **"**

boundary, no ethnic limitation, and no social barrier. It is something to practice, is acceptable, and the result is the same everywhere. Like the law of time and season; it affects everyone and everything; and everyone and everything respects the rule. The Bible is the book of general rules for all who believe. And all the examples will produce the same results anytime and anywhere they are followed. I often say to my brethren, "If what is said to one cannot be said to all, what is said to one should not be said at all." The gospel is the universal law of liberty. And giving glory to God is a scriptural example to be followed by whoever wants to experience the fulfilment of prophecy.

✡

GIVING GLORY TO GOD:

Call it praise, thanksgiving, or worship; it's all about giving glory to God. Thanksgiving, praise and worship are examples in scriptures you must follow to experience the fulfilment of prophecy. There is nothing like bad or good praise, worship, and thanksgiving. If it's praise, it's praise. If it's not praise, it's not. Giving glory to God is one of the general rules in scriptures practiced by the first prophet, Abraham.

"Yet he did not waver through unbelief regarding the promise of God, but was strengthened in his faith and gave glory to God." (Rom.4:20)

Every prophecy or promise from God, when understood, motivates a person to give glory to God. Even when the prophecy was delayed, Abraham kept praising God. Abraham knew that God values praise because it's one thing God can't do for Himself. When you praise God, you are expressing your faith in God's faithfulness. Praise is a way to remind God of His promise towards you. It's what you do while you await the manifestation of what is promised. Praise is focusing on the promise giver. When you praise God for the promise, He will turn it to a testimony because God dwells where there is praise (See Ps. 22:3).

Thanksgiving is the password to God's presence and in His presence there is fullness of everything. *"Enter with the password: 'Thank you!' Make yourselves at home, talking praise. Thank him. Worship him"* (Ps.100:4 MSG). While you thank God for what He has done, you praise Him for what He can and will do, and you worship Him for who He is. Thanksgiving, Praise, and worship can be done through dance, songs/music, words, in the Spirit (speaking in tongues), shouting, offering of substance, and offering of your body. It could either be organized with melody, or not organized without melody-joyful noise. Praise is telling of His goodness. It's celebrating His ability and faithfulness. Grumbling, which leads to destruction, is the opposite of praise. Those who grumbled were destroyed in the wilderness. Only the praisers entered the

> **"** When you praise God for the promise, He will turn it to a testimony because God dwells where there is praise... **"**

Promised Land as prophesied. The wall that separated the people from the fulfilment of prophecy collapsed when they praised (Josh.6:20). We are therefore warned not to grumble, but be thankful in all circumstances. "Praise" is the Master Key that opens the door to the supernatural.

Praise is Jesus' formula for solving difficult equations. When there was no bread to feed his followers; the bible said Jesus knew what he would do. He knows the formula to apply.

> *When Jesus looked up and saw a great crowd coming toward him, he said to Philip, "Where shall we buy bread for these people to eat?" He asked this only to test him, for he already had in mind what he was going to do... Jesus then took the loaves, gave thanks, and distributed to those who were seated as much as they wanted. He did the same with the fish. When they had all had enough to eat, he said to his disciples, "Gather the pieces that are left over. Let nothing be wasted." (John 6:5-12)*

At the tomb of Lazarus; Jesus applied the same formula of praise. *"So they took away the stone. Then Jesus looked up and said, 'Father, I thank you that you have heard me'"* (John 11:41).

Answers to prayers could be delayed by demons as seen in Dan.10:12-13, but God does not commit answers to praise to the angels. He responds promptly and personally.

> *A Gentile woman who lived there came to him, pleading, "Have mercy on me, O Lord, Son of David! For my daughter is possessed by a demon that*

torments her severely." But Jesus gave her no reply, not even a word. Then his disciples urged him to send her away. "Tell her to go away," they said. "She is bothering us with all her begging." Then Jesus said to the woman, "I was sent only to help God's lost sheep—the people of Israel." But she came and worshiped him, pleading again, "Lord, help me!" Jesus responded, "It isn't right to take food from the children and throw it to the dogs." She replied, "That's true, Lord, but even dogs are allowed to eat the scraps that fall beneath their masters' table." Dear woman," Jesus said to her, "your faith is great. Your request is granted." And her daughter was instantly healed." (Matt.15:22-28)

In this account, it seems this woman was ignored until she switched to praise.

The very first service we had in our ministry was a praise service. On that day, God said to us: "when you pray, you invite me to donate to you; when you worship me, you invite me, and to honor me. But when you invite me for honor, I will never leave you without donating to you." Ever since, in addition to special Praise services, we set aside a particular month for praise every year.

Does it look like God is not hearing or answering your prayers? It is time to switch to praise like the gentile woman. Whatever is worth praying for; is worth praising for. *"By him therefore let us offer the sacrifice of praise to God continually, that is, the fruit of our lip giving thanks to his name"* (Heb. 13:15; 2Chr 20:21-29).

Against the popular saying that every asset has a liability, 'Praise' is the force that has no disadvantages. I call it the master key because it opens all doors, flips all gates, and collapses walls. Praise can be done any way, anytime, and anywhere. It cannot be done wrongly.

"Let the message of Christ dwell among you richly as you teach and admonish one another with all wisdom through psalms, hymns, and songs from the Spirit, singing to God with gratitude in your hearts And whatever you do, whether in word or deed, do it all in the name of the Lord Jesus, giving thanks to God the Father through him." (Col.3:16-17)

> ❝ 'Praise' is the force that has no disadvantages...the master key because it opens all doors, flips all gates, and collapses walls. Praise can be done any way, anytime, and anywhere. ❞

Offerings and sacrifices could be rejected by God (Gen. 4:5); but not praise. Prayer could be an abomination before God; but not praise. Prayer without thanksgiving and praise can easily be turned into complaining and murmuring without knowing (Phil. 4:6). Therefore, if you pray for and over issues, it is time to praise for and over the same issues. Like the gentile woman, Praise disqualifies her disqualifiers and qualifies her for God's blessings. Cultivate the habit of always giving God glory. Praise God for your expectations, dreams and desires and you will not only see the manifestations, you will have the joy to avert murmuring while you wait for the manifestations. When giving glory to God becomes your habit, miracles become your lifestyle.

Follow The Example: Keep Giving Glory To God. ▪

> God wants us to learn how to use our pains for gain. We can use adversity for advantage. The trials we overcome today will become our testimonies tomorrow. And the word of our testimony is the weapon to overcome the devil himself

Thank you for taking time to read this book.
We trust you have been tremendously blessed.
Do you have any question?
Need counsel and prayers, or simply want to request additional copies or order some ministry materials?
Do not hesitate to reach us at any of the following addresses below.

KINGDOM AGENDA CHURCH
BALTIMORE MD 21229, USA
EMAIL: Philmosys07@gmail.com

KINGSWORLD INT'L MINISTRY
NO: 1 BETTER LIFE ARENA,
EVBUOTUBU 4 JUNCTION ,
BENIN CITY, EDO STATE, NIGERIA.
TEL: +2347033314606
EMAIL: philmosys07@gmail.com

Made in the USA
Middletown, DE
14 January 2020